What people are saying about
Taming the Paper Tiger at Home

"A 'must read' for anyone who spends more than five minutes a day shuffling paper."
KENNETH H. BLANCHARD
Co-Author of *The One Minute Manager*

"The top of my desk was like Jimmy Hoffa. It disappeared long ago. But thanks to Barbara Hemphill, what was lost has been found. Finally, I'm organized!"
BEVERLY BECKHAM
Columnist, *Boston Herald*

"Bravo for Barbara Hemphill's two-question test of a system: Does it work and do you like it? *Taming the Paper Tiger at Home* helps me find the joy in organizing. It works and I love it! It makes a great gift."
MAGGIE BEDROSIAN
Author, *Life is More Than Your To Do List*

"Barbara Hemphill's valuable, sensible, organizing techniques will help improve the quality of life in every home. This practical guide makes life easier for parents and children—now and in the years to come."
NANCY SAMALIN
Author, *Loving Your Child is Not Enough;*
Love and Anger: The Parental Dilemma and
Loving Without Spoiling

"Some of us in the creative arts (and we know who we are!) are not exactly born organizers when it comes to the tedious details of our lives. Lack of organization, while often charmingly Bohemian, can become a distraction that interferes with our creative processes if we let it get out of hand. The Paper Tiger methodology frees us from those distractions so we can focus more fully on what we do best—being creative!"
LANI SMITH
Composer

"I've been selling Barbara Hemphill's books for years. They seem to fly out of the store, and I know they're put to good use—my customers come back and rave that her sensible organizing ideas have changed their lives."

NANCY OLSON
Owner, Quail Ridge Books and
Independent Bookseller of the Year 2001

"My busy life as a United States ambassador was made much easier thanks to Barbara Hemphill's valuable advice on how to organize the masses of diplomatic and personal paper surrounding me. I still keep *Taming the Paper Tiger at Home* handy in my home."

PATRICIA GATES LYNCH
U.S. Ambassador (Retired)

"When I heard Barbara discussing *Taming the Paper Tiger at Home* on television, I got off my treadmill and started cleaning off my desk. For four years I had been looking for the missing link to start my business, and using Barbara's techniques, I discovered exactly what I needed! I owe it all to her. Whenever I practice "The Art of Wastebasketry," I think to myself, "Barbara would be so proud of me!" It makes such a difference in my life."

PAT BENDER
President, Bailey and Bender
Personal and Organization Development

"As a freelance writer and researcher, retrieving information is not only important, it is vital to me. For years I have been searching for one simple system that would allow me to retrieve the information I needed when I needed it. You have created that system! Your system is easy, simple and makes a big difference in how I do business. Kudos!"

CRIS J. BAKER ROBINS
Freelance writer

"This book has changed my life!"

SHARON MYERS
Mary Kay Cosmetics Consultant

Taming
the
Paper Tiger
at Home

Taming
the
Paper Tiger
at Home

BARBARA HEMPHILL
America's Favorite Professional Organizer

KIPLINGER BOOKS
Washington, DC

Published by
The Kiplinger Washington Editors, Inc.
1729 H Street, N.W.
Washington, D.C. 20006

Library of Congress Cataloging-in-Publication Data

Hemphill, Barbara.
    Taming the paper tiger at home/ Barbara Hemphill.--6th ed.
        p. cm.
    At head of title: Kiplinger's.
    Includes index.
    ISBN 0-938721-97-6(pbk.)
        1. Paperwork (Office practice)--Management. 2. Filing systems. I. Title.

HF5547.15 .H448 2002
640--dc21

                                                2002075422

This publication is intended to provide guidance in regard to the subject matter covered. It is sold with the understanding that the author and publisher are not herein engaged in rendering legal, accounting, tax or other professional services. If such services are required, professional assistance should be sought.

Sixth edition. Printed in the United States of America.

9 8 7 6 5 4 3 2 1

Acknowledgments

I first shared my dream of writing this book with Florence Feldman in 1982. Her professional expertise and her personal friendship are more valuable to me as the years go by.

There were literally hundreds of clients and friends who contributed to this book, not only with specific paper-management ideas, but with their ongoing interest and efforts on my behalf.

I especially want to thank David Harrison, Director of Kiplinger Books, for his continuing enthusiasm for my ideas, Cindy Greene, who provided logistical support, Allison Leopold for her meticulous proofreading, and Heather Waugh, who created the book's design.

My special appreciation to my personal assistant, DJ Watson, and her able team, whose varied talents greatly increased the quality of this book, and to Brooke Ballantyne, my home-office manager who continually enhances the quality of my personal and professional life.

Finally, I am especially thankful for the love and support of my husband, Alfred Taylor, who is the greatest fan club any writer ever had, and with whom I am enjoying being a grandparent!

Contents

PART TWO: Strategies for Paper Management

Introduction

I am often asked how I happened to write this book. The answer begins back in 1978, shortly after I moved to New York City after living overseas for eight years.

In searching for a way to make money and care for three children, I discovered what many others have: Successful businesses are often a result of a person identifying a need and filling it.

My discovery came while I was sitting at a playground commiserating with other parents. I'd hear comments such as, "I've just got to get organized." "We haven't eaten on the dining room table in a month. It's covered with paper!" or "I don't even like to go to the mailbox. I don't know what to do with all that junk." I became acutely aware that many people had difficulty "getting organized," and that "getting organized" had always been one of my strengths. So I put an ad in the neighborhood newspaper, and the phone started ringing within a few days. Then, while looking for resources for my clients, I discovered that there was no book written on how to manage paper. Hence, *Taming the Paper Tiger at Home* was born. (A companion book, *Taming the Paper Tiger at Work*, followed a few years later. It's also published by Kiplinger Books.)

Perhaps my greatest fear in writing this book has been that as people read examples of how I "tame my paper tiger," they'll think, "But I could never be as good as she is!" Rest assured that I am not always able to do all of the things you'll read about. I don't think anyone can. But I think you can benefit from what's written here.

Much of my advice comes from my own experiences, both professional and personal. Before I became an organizational consultant, I held several different jobs (paid and volunteer) and entertained extensively for my husband's organization. I have been divorced—and learned to deal with issues peculiar to a single-parent family—and remarried to a man with two children of his own, thus providing me with the opportunity to experience the rigors of managing a blended family. Through all of this, I've been active in my church and professional and community organizations. So one way or another, I've probably had to deal personally with some aspect of paper management in which you're interested.

This book is meant to be a reference that you can use time and again, as you require new or revised paper-management systems. In addition to the information available here, you will also need to add time, patience and practice. After all, very few problems are resolved by simply reading a book!

Feel free to use the book, which has ample room for you to make notes in the margins. I've selected short bits of advice, mottos and other things for you to think about as you develop your paper-management system, and scattered them through the margins. Also, underline or highlight as you read; turn down page corners that particularly interest you. Contrary to what you may have been taught, I can assure you that nothing makes a writer happier than a well-worn book!

One of the most exciting results of publishing this book has been talking to hundreds of people who are "taming their paper tiger." As I travel around the country, I hear about the experiences of readers experimenting with new ways to handle the paper blizzard. One of my favorite remarks is from a reader in Florida who wrote, "I have spent my entire life stepping over boxes and bags of paper. I have tamed not only the tiger, but his offspring as well!"

There is another side to the story. Many of the letters and phone calls I receive are from people whose lives, or the lives of people they love, are nearly paralyzed by paper. They need additional help. The chapter "Paperholics" provides some suggestions.

"Organized" is not a destination, but a journey. It's not about perfectionism, but progress. Sometimes the road is long and rough. I have tried to write this book as though you were in the room with me and we were working together, one on one.

When I wrote the first version of *Taming the Paper Tiger*, in 1988, many people expressed concern that with the advent of the computer, people wouldn't be very interested in the topic of "paper taming." In reality, we're now faced with even more paper, and in addition, we have to tame our computers!

I believe that the problem of managing the paper that comes into our lives has grown far more serious. With more dual-career and single-parent families, as well as families caring for aging parents, the challenges are growing. Not only is there more to organize than ever, but the price for not being able to find what you need when you want it can range from simply frustrating to catastrophic.

One of the things that most distresses me is how unwilling people are to ask for help in getting organized. I have clients who agonized for years before they finally decided to call us. There are a variety of reasons for their hesitation—among them is embarrassment. After all, they are very successful, intelligent, famous, rich, poor—the list goes on. Dozens of people have described situations where the only thing that made them take the plunge was the devastating effect their disorganization was having on a relationship.

Based on the feedback I've had from thousands of readers, I know that the techniques described in this book are even more relevant today than they were in the past, and that implementing them will make a difference in the quality of your life.

We realize that as soon as you hold this book in your hands, it is possible that some of my resource recommendations may be outdated or upgraded. I encourage you to visit my website at www.ProductiveEnvironment.com and go to the Taming the Paper Tiger Home page, where we post updates and additional useful information.

As you use this book and have questions or ideas or would like information about consulting services or seminars, please feel free to contact me at:

Hemphill Productivity Institute, Inc.
1464 Garner Station Boulevard, #330
Raleigh, NC 27603-3634
919-773-0722
barbara@ProductiveEnvironment.com

Barbara Hemphill
Summer 2002

The Paper-Management System

CHAPTER 1

The Roar of the Tiger

Whether you're male or female, young or old, make $30,000 a year and live in a studio apartment or make $300,000 a year and live on a ten-acre estate, you are, or will be, deluged with paper.

Do you recognize this scene? You sit down to pay some bills. You know the electric bill needs to be paid, but you can't remember where you put it. Your son comes in to tell you he needs his birth certificate the next day to prove he's old enough for driving lessons. Where is it? Your friend calls to ask if you're free on the eighteenth for a get-together. That date stands out in your mind for some reason. You think maybe there's a notation on your calendar at work, but there's nothing on your home calendar.

You feel a headache coming on. There are piles of bills, junk mail and catalogs all over your desk and night table and the piles seem to grow before your eyes!

What you're experiencing is the roar of the tiger—the paper tiger.

You may feel like the tiger's out of control, that the situation is hopeless. The truth is, you can stop this pattern—tame that tiger—with a powerful tool: a paper-management system.

A paper-management system is a tool to help you accomplish what is important to you, whether it's finding your birth certificate when you need it, paying your bills on time, having all the papers you need when you go to your tax accountant, submitting insurance claims within the time limit, or keeping track of your frequent-flier miles.

As an organizing consultant, I've spent thousands of hours working with people and their paper, from parents struggling with the piles of papers their kids bring home from school to corporate executives responsible for thousands of files. One fact is absolutely clear: Paper-management skills are essential to survive the information explosion in our society.

A Profusion of Paper

The sheer volume of mail that we confront daily demands increased skills in paper management. Compare the amount of mail in your mailbox today with that of five years ago. And while the computer age was billed as the "paperless age," it didn't take any of us long to realize that, although the computer does eliminate some piles of paper, it can also create even larger piles. People often say they hate paper. If so, why do they have so much trouble getting rid of it? How many people print out that important e-mail message—or the information gathered from a great Web site—often for no good reason? Computers have an increasing impact on our lives; learning to manage the paper they generate is essential.

Deciding what to do with catalogs is a major issue in many households. Our fascination with sleek, alluring ads for products to improve our appearance, reduce our workload or please our family, plus our inability to decide whether we are buying or browsing, adds piles of catalogs in many places around the house. And don't forget all those magic money-saving offers. Rarely does a day go by without the arrival of at least one "Have we got a deal for you!" or an offer of a special rate for a new credit card.

Another major contributor to the paper pile-up is the photocopy machine. Most of us have easy access to a machine in our workplace, at the local library or at the neighborhood convenience store—and for more and more of us, right in our own home. We cut out articles, advertisements, recipes, and book reviews we think will interest a family member or a friend, and make a copy—and an extra . . . just in case. Then we have to decide where to keep our own copy, and how to get the other copies to the intended recipients. Unless you have a system to accomplish that task easily, the results over a period of months or years can be devastating. You can wind up with piles and shopping bags full of good intentions stuffed under beds and in closets, boxes stacked in the attic or basement, and drawers badly needed for current storage of essentials, filled instead with unidentified papers.

Changing Family Lifestyles

Another complicating factor in managing paper today is the basic change in family lifestyle. Dad used to sit down at his desk at the end of each month to pay the bills. He probably never had more than five or six—in a busy month!

Now, with companies offering financial savings with the use of their own credit cards, the number of bills to pay each month has increased substantially. In single-parent or dual-income families, the time for paper shuffling is limited, but the amount of paper to shuffle seems unlimited: child-care arrangements, car-pool schedules, travel itineraries, shopping lists, school permission slips, house repair to-do lists, and piles of career-related magazines and newspapers to read. Support from family members—and from household and personal services—is vital, but using it effectively requires good paper-management skills.

Blended families with children from more than one marriage also create special paper-management challenges. If you're divorced, for example, and need to take your son to buy soccer shoes, but you see him only on Tuesday night, you need a system that makes you see your reminder to "buy soccer shoes on Tuesday." It won't help to see the reminder on Wednesday.

I grew up on a farm in Nebraska. I remember that as a young girl learning to cook, I quickly discovered that while it was quite simple to make every dish on the dinner menu, the hard part was getting them all on the table at the same time, with the potatoes and gravy hot, the rolls warm and the salad still molded. That was the real challenge! Paper management requires that same skill.

Most people know how to do most of the individual

Your ability to accomplish any task is directly related to your ability to find the right thing at the right time — and frequently it's on paper.

tasks required in personal paper-management—paying bills, writing letters, filing papers, etc. The difficult part is getting it all done at the right time. To accomplish that requires a comprehensive system.

This book provides guidelines to help you fill in the gaps in your paper-management system, or to develop a totally new one if you feel it's necessary. The principles I discuss often apply to your electronic world as well.

Developing a personal paper-management system takes motivation, time and practice. If you've been shuffling the same piles of paper for months, or even years, it will take time to change, and it can be frightening. Accept this as a "normal" reaction, not an indication that you are doing something wrong.

Digging through a pile of papers can be compared to waking a sleeping tiger. We discover papers that represent disappointments, obligations, uncertainty, indecision and the blinding reality that we are not able to do all the things we want to or think we ought to. Just as we have a temporary respite when the tiger sleeps, we have a temporary respite when we ignore the papers, but constantly in the back of our minds is the fear that the tiger will awaken.

The results of organizing the paper in your life will be more than just uncluttered counters. As one client put it, "I was so preoccupied with finding my way through the forest that I didn't notice the trees. Organizing my paper made it easier for me to identify what is important in my life." An effective paper-management system will help you control what you do with your time and energy and create an environment that is supportive of your plans and dreams.

I don't believe that we ever set goals that are too high. We just allow too little time to reach them. Suppose you decide you want to learn to play tennis. You can buy the best book on the subject, get the best coach, the latest equipment, the most fashionable clothing and go to the best court, but you won't be an expert tennis player after a few hours; it takes time and practice. Learning paper-management skills also takes time, like learning any other skill, but you can do it—and it will be worth the effort!

Answer the Tiger's Roar

Paper management means creating—and sustaining—a system that fits your personal needs. No matter what your paper-management challenges are, there's a way for you to improve the way you handle paper—one that works for your own needs and lifestyle. You may know how to handle a particular paper problem, but for various reasons you have not done so. Before long, the paper gets lost in the shuffle of more papers. You become so bogged down in all this paper that you end up not taking the appropriate action to end the vicious cycle.

Successful paper management requires five basic ingredients:

1. Clear picture of desired results
2. Positive attitude
3. Sufficient time
4. Appropriate tools
5. Regular maintenance

If any component of the system is weak or missing, the system will begin to break down. Nine times out of ten, when a system breaks down, it is a sign of a changing situation, not a bad system. Perhaps the amount of paper has grown, the support system has changed, or the objectives have been revised.

A Clear Picture

The first question I frequently ask a client is "What would success look like?" or "What will you be able to do when you are organized that you are not doing now?" Organization in and of itself has no value—it is simply a tool to help you do what you want to do. The clearer you are about what you want to do, the more effectively you can get organized.

Getting organized is not about becoming a neat freak—unless, of course, you want to—or about doing things the way someone else does. My definition of organization is very simple: Does it work? Do you like it? And if what you organize—or don't organize—affects others, then you should ask a third question, "Does it work for others?"

Think Positively

A positive attitude as it relates to paper management is an essential prerequisite. It is important for you to expect that, with the help of this book, you can and will develop a system that will suit your particular needs.

One of the most exciting aspects of being an organizing consultant is helping people create a system, then seeing their sense of relief when they realize how much simpler their lives can be. Frequently, people procrastinate about doing anything with the paper in their lives because they are waiting to find the "right" way.

There is no right or wrong way. Many times I set up systems for other people that I personally would find very frustrating. As you read this book you will discover that there are many styles of paper management. Don't worry about how other people do it. Just look for techniques that work for you. What you choose to do with a piece of paper is not nearly as important as doing it consistently.

To foster your positive attitude about paper management, recognize that any system you develop is a tool to help you do what you want or need to do. A friend of mine says, "I hate jogging; I love having jogged!" Paperwork is like that in many ways. Few people like doing it, but taking the time to set up a system means spending less time shuffling paper and more time enjoying the results—in short, taming the paper tiger.

Tomorrow and Tomorrow and Tomorrow

How many times have you said to yourself: "I'll get organized when things calm down/after I write the report for my boss/when the kids go back to school/when the kids get out of school/after the guests leave/when I come home from my business trip/when the house is remodeled/as soon as I have a block of time—this weekend maybe, or over the holidays/when I'm on vacation/when I retire/tomorrow."

But the weekend, the holidays, the vacations come and go. As soon as one crisis is over (and sometimes before), another begins. Before you know it, you have a desk full of letters you really intended to answer and ten months of health insurance claims to submit. The attic and basement are filled with magazines you never read while they were in the den (but that contain wonderful articles and recipes). And it's April 10th, and you have no idea where your income-tax forms are stashed. Many a client has called after being retired for several months, or even years, saying "I still don't have the time."

If you wait "until things calm down" before you do something about the paper tiger in your life, it could be a very long wait.

Decide to Decide

There is a very simple axiom regarding paper: Paper clutter is postponed decisions; paper management is making decisions.

Papers pile up on our counters, tables and desks because there are decisions we need to make about them. "Do I really need to keep this letter from my lawyer about my father's estate?" "Where should I keep my will?" "What do I do with all those family photographs my mother gave me for safekeeping?" "How can I find that recipe I saw in *Gourmet* magazine when I want it?" "What should I do with health insurance statements?" "Where do I put the operating instructions for the new garage-door opener?"

What you choose to do with a piece of paper is not nearly as important as doing it consistently.

Paper itself is not the problem. Paper is a symptom of a problem.

Paper itself is not the problem. Paper is a symptom of a problem. Every time you ask one of the above questions without making a reply—a decision—and then taking the appropriate action, you have left some unsettled business. Postpone a few of the decisions, and a new pile is born.

Four Questions to Ask About Every Piece of Paper

1. Do I really need to keep this?
2. Where should I keep it?
3. How long should I keep it?
4. How can I find it?

Each of these questions requires making a decision. But many people run into trouble here. Why are these decisions so difficult for us to make? There are two major reasons—lack of information and fear of failure.

Information, Please

Even though paper management is an essential skill in the twenty-first century, few people have had an opportunity to learn these skills in a formal way. It simply is not taught.

The purpose of this book is to help you recognize the paper-management problems in your life, to motivate you to do something about them, and to provide you with the tools to find solutions and develop systems.

The place to begin is with the questionnaire on pages 12 and 13, which I developed as the starting point for my clients. So get a pencil and let's get going!

Each chapter is complete within itself. You do not need to read the entire book to be able to put it to work for you, but do read the entire chapter before you begin trying a new system. Use this as a reference book, not only when you are first setting up a system, but to refer to as you outgrow existing systems and find you need to make revisions.

But . . . What If?

Fear is a big reason people have difficulty deciding what to do with their papers. You're afraid that your decision will be proved wrong, you'll regret your decision, or that someone will be disappointed or hurt by your decision. You ask yourself: "What if I get audited by the IRS and I don't have what I need?" "What if I throw something away and it turns out to be very valuable?" "What if my children want or need this information someday?" "What if I file this important document and then I can't find it?"

It's not easy to answer the "what ifs" correctly. Most of us have, at one time or another, thrown out something we wind up needing later on. But here are the facts: 1) If your paper tiger is big enough, you can't find most of your paper anyway; and 2) almost everything is replaceable. You can probably get another copy if you really need to, and,if you don't really need to, then it probably wasn't worth the clutter it would have caused in the first place. Here's what I call Hemphill's Principle: "If you don't know you have it, or you can't find it, it is of NO value to you!"

No Magic in Insight

Suppose you can take the time to set up a system, and you know what you need to do, but you just don't want to do it? What then?

There is no magic in insight! Just because you know there is a better way doesn't mean you will do it. You need to take action on your insight. I know that if I exercise at least twenty minutes a day, three times a week, I will feel better, look better and live longer—but that in itself does not make me ride my bicycle or jog.

In fact, we frequently do not act on our insights—until a crisis forces us to do so. We become concerned about our eating habits when the doctor says our life is at risk if we do not. Similarly, we decide to do something about a cluttered desk when we recognize that it doesn't work for us anymore. One client of mine decided to do

continued on page 14

Fear is a big reason people have difficulty deciding what to do with their papers.

PAPER-MANAGEMENT SKILLS SURVEY

When I meet with a new client, the first thing I do is ask the client to fill out this questionnaire to determine what areas of paper management need work. Evaluate the following statements yourself. Any statement that gets a 3 or higher indicates an area where you need help. The right-hand column tells which chapter to turn to.

Strongly Agree = 1 **Agree** = 2 **Uncertain** = 3 **Disagree** = 4 **Strongly Disagree** = 5

Issue	Rating	See Chapter
I have an accessible and comfortable place in my home where I do paperwork.	1 2 3 4 5	3
I have the "paper-management tools" (stationery, office supplies, etc.) that I need.	1 2 3 4 5	3
I have a calendar system that works for me and my family.	1 2 3 4 5	7
I can easily find names, addresses and phone numbers when I need them.	1 2 3 4 5	9
I have a bill-paying system that works for me.	1 2 3 4 5	13
I have a filing system that works for me and can be used by others if necessary.	1 2 3 4 5	10
I can find family records (medical, educational, etc.) whenever I need them.	1 2 3 4 5	17
I am comfortable with my record of charitable donations.	1 2 3 4 5	13
I am confident my tax records are adequate for the IRS.	1 2 3 4 5	14
I keep good records of household and automobile repairs and maintenance.	1 2 3 4 5	10
I have a large wastebasket I can reach when doing my paperwork.	1 2 3 4 5	3
I can find warranties and directions for appliances when I need them.	1 2 3 4 5	17
I have a comfortable place to use my computer.	1 2 3 4 5	3

Issue	Rating	See Chapter
I am comfortable with my records of magazine and newspaper subscriptions.	1 2 3 4 5	22
I am comfortable with the newspapers and magazines around my house.	1 2 3 4 5	15
I like the way my recipes are organized.	1 2 3 4 5	19
I have enough space for books and can find one when I want or need it.	1 2 3 4 5	3
I organize my photographs and other family memorabilia to my satisfaction.	1 2 3 4 5	18
I can easily reach the telephone when I am working.	1 2 3 4 5	3
I am comfortable with the amount of time I spend retrieving information.	1 2 3 4 5	10
I can find the information I called about when my phone call is returned.	1 2 3 4 5	11
I have a "To Do" list system that works for me.	1 2 3 4 5	8
I take some action on a piece of paper every time I pick it up.	1 2 3 4 5	5
I am comfortable with the amount of paper I throw away or recycle.	1 2 3 4 5	6
I keep up with my correspondence to my satisfaction.	1 2 3 4 5	16
I can find travel information or records whenever I want them.	1 2 3 4 5	21
I am comfortable with the way I handle my children's records and memorabilia.	1 2 3 4 5	20
I could find the papers I want to take with me if I had to evacuate my house.	1 2 3 4 5	12

something about his paper tiger when the penalty on his overdue inheritance-tax bill became larger than his annual income and he was threatened with jail! What price are you willing to pay before you act?

Ultimately you will have to make the decision to tame the tiger yourself. The most I can do is point out how chaotic the alternative is and show you ways to create a system that works for you. No doubt you know that already, or you wouldn't be reading this. *Taming the Paper Tiger at Home* will give you answers to questions and guidelines to use that will help you form your own system for managing the paper tiger in your life. The rest is up to you.

CHAPTER 3

Get Centered

t's Monday. You arrive home from work or from the afternoon soccer carpool feeling exhausted and rushed to get to a 7:30 P.M. meeting. You grab the mail out of the box and glance at it while you drink a quick cup of coffee.

You begin making piles on the kitchen table: one for trash because there isn't a wastebasket within reach; one for bills you need to pay; another for things you want to read. Before you can get through all the mail, the phone rings. You answer it. By the time you finish your conversation, it's time for dinner. You scoop everything up— trash and all, since there isn't time to determine which pile is which—and put it in the bay window.

On Tuesday you sit down in the family room to read the mail. The children are watching TV, and you want to spend a little time with them before dinner. The routine is the same as the day before. You get distracted. But this time the pile goes on the coffee table.

On Wednesday the mail winds up on the table beside your bed because you want to talk to your spouse before your business trip.

By the end of the week, you have several piles of mail around the house, half-opened, half-read and cluttering every room. But you can't find the bill you planned to pay yesterday or the tickets that you need for the game tonight!

Just as no business can run smoothly without an office, no household can run smoothly without an office to coordinate "the business of life." So the first step in solving your paper-management problem at home is to establish a location where you will routinely handle all your paperwork. (You might already have a location, but the paper may hide it. If so, keep reading.) If you want to tame that tiger, you have to start by putting him in a cage.

I strongly urge you to set up a permanent center for your paperwork that will be available to you at all times. At seminars I give for managing paper at the office, one of the most frequent comments I hear from participants is, "It's even worse at home!" I ask them, "Where do you do your paperwork at home?" Typically, the response is "sometimes here . . . sometimes there."

Therein lies a major part of the problem. It fascinates me that while nearly everyone has a specific location in their home devoted to the preparation of food, far fewer people have a specific location devoted to the handling of paper. Yet most people spend as much or more time handling paper than they do preparing food.

Just taking your mail to a central place will eliminate scattered piles of paper, misplaced bills and checks, and forgotten notices. One seminar participant was amazed at how much easier her life became once she established a work area in the kitchen with a desk, a telephone and a file cabinet.

"How can that be so important?" you may ask. Have you ever tried to repot a plant in the kitchen sink using a tablespoon because you didn't feel like going out to the garage to get the proper tool? Have you ever ruined an expensive suit by trying to remove a spot on the jacket when you didn't have the proper cleaner? It's no different from the many times you opened an invitation to a party that you wouldn't dream of missing, but procrastinated about RSVPing because the telephone was in the other room. Have you mailed a bill a week later than you planned to because you kept forgetting to buy stamps?

When I was growing up on the family farm in Nebraska, my father used to tell me that half the battle in getting any job done is having the right tool. (I've since adapted the saying: "Half of any job is using the right tool!") The same is true in paper management.

Choose Your Paper Place

The first thing to consider in choosing a place for handling your papers is choosing a place you like. If you like sunshine or have allergies to mold, an unfinished, dark basement is not likely to be satisfactory. If you like to be in the mainstream of family activity, the family room may be an excellent location. But maybe you're easily distracted, or you'd like a quiet place to go to after a hectic day at the office. Then an out-of-the-way bedroom or a study will probably work better. If you have small children, you could set up your work center in an area where they can play while you work.

Paperwork under the best of circumstances isn't much fun, and you won't be encouraged to do it if you dislike your work area. So do whatever you can to make it a place you like to be. Get a radio or CD player if you like music; put a cushion on your chair; or get a new lamp to put on your desk.

Many people would rather not set aside a separate space for a work area, preferring to use the kitchen or dining-room table. Others have no option because of space constraints. For these situations, I recommend a mobile bill-paying center that can be housed in a portable file box, basket or rolling file. Check your local office-supply or discount department store for wonderful examples. However, if at all possible, establish a permanent location that can be used exclusively for managing your paper. You don't want to have to constantly interrupt the bill-paying process because the table has to be cleared and set for dinner.

A Desk Is a Desk Is a Desk... Or Is It?

Does it matter what type of desk or desk arrangement you designate for your work center? You bet it does! Some desks simply will not work for you. The key word is "functional."

Many homes have desks that are lovely to look at

The first consideration for your paper-management center is choosing a place you like.

and horrible to use. A rolltop desk, for example, while very beautiful, is difficult for most people to use because of the limited workspace, and the numerous cubbyholes soon become catch-alls for unidentified papers. If you are going to use such a desk, be sure to label the various compartments: one for envelopes, one for bills, one for stamps, and so on.

A NOTE ABOUT SHARING

Although our parents taught us that sharing was an admirable thing, when it comes to a desk, it is seldom workable unless both partners are really willing to work at it. Sharing a desk requires communication, flexibility, and discipline. It's often easier and more effective to create a second workspace, giving the most desirable spot to the person who spends the most time at the desk.

Some people love those beautiful secretary desks—love to look at them, that is. The biggest disadvantage to this type of desk is its small size. The best way to use a secretary is to designate it for a particular paper project, such as personal correspondence. If you are particularly fond of the desk or it has sentimental significance, this will be an advantage. You will like to go there, and you will therefore be more inclined to write personal letters. Keep all your notepaper and stationery there, or at least a supply of any different styles you may use, as well as any greeting cards you have purchased. Put letters you want to answer in one spot. When the pile starts to build up, you know it's time to make an appointment with yourself to write letters. Put your favorite picture postcards there as well. You will be able to answer a letter, write a quick thank you note, or send a birthday card in the five minutes you have before the taxi comes or before you drive the carpool.

One of my clients had four desks and none of them worked. Her first assignment was to choose the one she liked most, get some boxes and empty the desk entirely. From that point, we started over to make not only a desk that she liked, but also a desk that worked.

Obviously, many of the decisions you make regarding your work area will be based on how much room you have in your home. But even if your space is limited there are numerous possibilities. In addition to checking out office-supply and discount department stores, used office-equipment centers often have some great bargains on high-quality furniture from companies that have moved or closed.

Many people are now using the computer to assist in the bill-paying process. There are wonderful, inexpensive and decorative computer stations available. Don't make the mistake of using an outdated desk for the computer—in order to enjoy the task and avoid injury, your station should be ergonomically sound. A monitor at eye level and a keyboard tray are minimal requirements for an effective computer station. Some of them close up like an armoire. When the work is done, your home becomes your home again—not an office.

Set Up Your Center

Wherever you choose to make your work area, be sure you have adequate lighting and a comfortable chair. One client and I spent a considerable amount of time setting up her paper-management system. She understood it and liked it, yet she never seemed to get things done—until we discovered the root of the problem. Her arthritic neck always hurt when she sat at the desk. As soon as we purchased an adjustable chair, the neck ache disappeared. When you adjust your chair, keep in mind that most experts agree that you want both feet planted firmly on the floor and your keyboard at a level where your elbows are parallel to the floor.

If you want to be able to move around in your work area, you will find a swivel chair on rollers a big advantage. If your area is carpeted, you will need an acrylic chair mat.

A major factor in managing paper is an effective filing system. (For a detailed discussion, see Chapter 10.) A file cabinet is one of the best investments you will ever make. It is ideal if some filing space is located at or close to your work center.

There is a variety of filing equipment on the market—other than the traditional metal file cabinet—ranging from inexpensive cardboard boxes to costly acrylic file cabinets on rollers. Rolling files are an excellent choice if you can't keep your files at your work area. You

Caution: Avoid allowing your bulletin board to become a catch-all for postponed decisions.

AN OFFICE IN A CLOSET

If you live in a small apartment, condominium or house, finding a place you can call your own to do paperwork may require some creative thinking. One client solved the problem by turning her front hall closet into an office so she could organize her paper as soon as she walked in the front door. She put in a small file cabinet, a large wastebasket, a bulletin board, and some "cubby holes" to sort her bills, reading material, filing etc. A counter-high table with a stool where she could sit to sort her mail completed the scene, and solved a problem she had struggled with for 20 years. The large double-door closets found in the bedrooms of many new homes work very well, and may be the perfect solution for you.

can move them to your workplace as you need them and roll them back out of the way when you're done. This is not time to skimp—make sure your filing cabinet has full-suspension drawers (some of the cheaper models do not). If you can't open the cabinet to its full extension, you will not be able to access the papers in the back, causing frustration, lost files and—worst of all—a broken filing system. Most types of files are found in office-supply stores and mail-order catalogs. Check in your local classified pages to see if there are office-furniture stores that sell quality "gently used" office equipment at affordable prices. My local office-furniture store even has a section of "experienced furniture." Not only does this meet the budget, the furniture apparently knows what to do!

If you have one computer in your home, decide whether it should be located in your work area or somewhere else, so that you can still work while other family members use the computer.

Have a telephone within easy reach of your work area, even if it means putting a 25-foot cord on the phone in the next room or buying a cordless phone. You will be amazed at how many pieces of paper you can eliminate immediately by making a phone call when you first open your mail.

If you are right-handed, you will probably want the phone on your left so that you're free to write while talking on the phone. If you're short on desk space, consider a wall phone, but be sure to get one with the buttons and the on/off switch on the handset so you can make several calls without having to get up from your desk. An answering machine, or answering service provided by your telephone company, is standard equipment for most homes.

You will need a To-Sort Tray (see Chapter 5) located on or within easy reach of your desk to collect the papers that require your action when you are ready to work. In addition, you will probably need an Out Tray for things you need to take other places, such as the post office, and a To-File Tray for papers that need to be filed in places you can't reach from your chair. You will probably also want an Action File (see Chapter 11).

Other pieces of equipment you may find helpful are a calculator, a postage scale and a bulletin board. Be careful about that last one—for many people, a bulletin board simply becomes a catch-all for postponed decisions. To avoid that, identify it for a specific purpose, such as for posting upcoming invitations, greeting cards, or other mementos you've received (to be changed when they become tired-looking), messages to family members, or an envelope system for credit-card receipts and bank-deposit records (see Chapter 13).

Last, but not least, a large wastebasket is one of the most important tools in your work area. I can't explain why, but I've observed that people are more likely to use a large wastebasket than a small one, so choose carefully. If you generate a lot of paper that is recyclable, consider two baskets, a large one for the paper and a smaller one for incidental waste. If you're concerned about confidentiality, a paper shredder is a great tool—and, as a bonus, the shredded paper makes great packing paper!

Basic Supplies

Once you have all the major equipment you need, make sure you have the necessary desk supplies. Nothing is more annoying than discovering you've run out of staples, or to find a bill you thought was paid a week ago buried in the bottom of your purse or briefcase because you didn't have a stamp when you needed it. You can order your stamps by mail now, so the next time you are running low, just leave a note and a check for your mail carrier. Or you can use an Internet postage service, such as www.stamps.com, to print your own postage and eliminate trips to the post office. A simple postal scale will be handy to have if you decide to go this route.

Be wary of clutter, such as pens that don't write well, paperweights you don't like or use, or drawers full of forgotten objects. If your desk is filled with such things, start over. Get a box and empty the contents of your desk, keeping only those items you use or enjoy seeing in your work area.

Check the list on the opposite page for ideas for organizing and stocking your work center.

If you have everything you feel you will need, the first step on the road to effective paper management is complete. Congratulations! That tiger will be purring in no time.

ESSENTIAL SUPPLIES FOR ANY OFFICE

Here's a checklist of supplies no well-organized office or work area should be without. What happens when you clip a magazine article for your files, and when you go to staple it you discover you are out? You're frustrated. You can make a special trip to get staples (a waste of time when you could have made one trip to pick up many supplies). Or you have to fold the corner together as a poor substitute for a staple (the pages fall apart). Wouldn't it be simpler to just make sure you have an extra box of staples?

Telephone. Obvious? Perhaps, but you have a variety of phone types and features to choose from, many of which could enhance productivity.

To-Sort Tray for items you haven't looked at. Don't let this tray get overloaded. When it is full you must pay attention to it. And do not submit to the temptation of buying a bigger tray.

Out Tray for items to be mailed or given to someone else.

To-File Tray for items to be filed in drawers you can't reach from your chair.

Action File to keep handy those items that will require action immediately or in the near future.

Container for writing utensils, unless you'd rather keep them in your drawer. In addition to pens and pencils, they should include:

- highlighter
- felt-tipped pen for handwriting labels
- thick marker for marking boxes
- different colored pens for calendar notations

Rotary card file and extra cards, unless you use a computer program or portable electronic organizer.

Calendar, paper or electronic

Stapler and staple remover

Labelmaker, worth considering for files, shelves and doors

Clock

Ruler

Magnifying glass, if you need to read very small print.

Stationery supplies, including:
- business-size stationery and envelopes
- mailing envelopes of various sizes
- postcards
- notecards
- adhesive notes
- return-address labels
- file folders and labels

Stamps

Tape

Scissors

Rubberbands

Paperclips and binderclips

Wastebasket/recycling box

The Keys to the System

Do you have drawers full of unidentified papers, shopping bags crammed with papers shoved under the bed, boxes overflowing with unread magazines stuffed in the closet? Perhaps you haven't eaten on the dining room table for a week because of the papers piled there. You want to end this vicious cycle, and you're encouraged by what you've read so far. But you're wondering where to begin.

Who's Controlling Whom?

A clean desk isn't important or necessary to everyone, but the ability to find information when you need it is. Perhaps you're afraid that if you file it, you'll forget what it is you need to do or never be able to find the papers again. Have you ever been late to an important engagement because the memo announcing it was not where you thought it was and you had to spend fifteen minutes looking for it? If so, then you're not controlling the paper—the paper is controlling you.

The solution is an effective paper-management system. But how do you develop one?

Paper piles indicate a pattern of postponed decisions. The paper-management system described in the next chapters will assist you in deciding where your paper should go and help you accomplish the following objectives:

- **Eliminate** unnecessary paper.
- **Avoid** generating unnecessary paper.

- **Establish** a location for essential paper.
- **Create** a method for easy retrieval of paper.

When you have no paper-management system or when the system you do have isn't working, the unavoidable problems of paper in the 21st Century are compounded. You soon discover that you are writing notes about notes you have already written because you are afraid you won't find the first one. Your calendar is bulging with notices of special events you're thinking of going to but you fail to find the notes until the event is over. You spend hours looking for that crucial piece of paper that you know you put someplace special but end up calling to get a duplicate because it is nowhere to be found.

Clutter is Postponed Decisions

Have you ever looked at a pile of papers and said, "OK, today's the day. I'm going to clean up this mess." You pick up the first piece of paper—and think of any number of reasons why today isn't a good day to deal with it. You pick up the second and the third—and before you know it, the pile that was on the left side of the table is now on the right. You've just experienced one of the major principles of organization: Clutter is postponed decisions. But I've got good news for you! There are only three decisions you can make about any piece of paper. To make it easier to remember, I call it The FAT System: File, Act, or Toss.

In my experience, every piece of paper in your life can be managed effectively by following The FAT System, which means putting any piece of paper, or the information on it, into one of seven places:

1. **To-Sort Tray**
2. **Wastebasket**
3. **Calendar**
4. **To-do list**
5. **Rotary telephone file or phone book**
6. **Reference File**
7. **Action File**

FORGET ABOUT THE BACKLOG

When I first started as an organizing consultant and was faced with a huge backlog of a client's papers, I thought that I should work with the client to eliminate that backlog first and then develop a system.

It didn't take long to realize that effective paper management means developing a system to stop feeling guilty over yesterday's pile and do something about today's. Instead of starting with the boxes that you never unpacked from your last move, last year's magazines that you never read, or even the unopened mail from last month, start with today's mail!

Perhaps you're saying to yourself, "That's far too regimented for me. I could never do that."

The fact is you can. I've worked with dozens of clients who thought my system would never work, but they discovered they can adapt it to meet their particular style.

Here's how it works: All the papers you decide to keep fall into one of two categories—action or reference. Action papers are those you need to do something about. The tools you use for them are your calendar, your to-do list and your Action Files. Reference papers contain information you want or need to keep for the future. The tools you use for those are your rotary telephone file or phone book and your Reference Files.

Imagine how it will feel to be able to clean off the kitchen counter when company is coming—and know that you will be able to find the credit-card bill again tomorrow. Think of how much frustration—and embarrassment—you'll avoid when you're able to spend two minutes retrieving the directions to a business meeting instead of fifteen minutes trying to reach your client to ask for them again.

You will discover that it is possible to control the paper in your life, and the rewards you'll get from taking control will greatly enhance the quality of your daily life.

Remember that today's mail is tomorrow's pile. Take today's mail to your paper-management center, and begin now to develop your own paper-management system.

Sort It Out

You may have heard the expression, "Handle a piece of paper only once." For the majority of the people I know, this is impossible. However, I think it is possible—and desirable— to handle a piece of paper only once more after it has been placed in a To-Sort Tray. Many people refer to this as their in-box, but I shy away from the term. Often people are not clear about the meaning of in, and I find mail weeks or even years old in the bottom of their in-box. Soon it becomes a hiding place for postponed decisions or undesirable tasks.

Paper should stay in your To-Sort Tray just long enough for you to determine what you need to do with it next, and that's where The FAT System comes in. You're either going to file the paper, act on it, or toss it. In some cases, it will go directly into the wastebasket (Chapter 6), or you will want to take immediate action, so one handling will be enough. But in many cases, you will move it from the To-Sort Tray into another part of your paper-management system. Chapters 7 through 11 describe in detail the five places your paper might belong in the system.

For many people, deciding where to begin is the biggest paper-management stumbling block. One day you look at the top of the desk and decide that the situation has gone far enough. You're tired of looking at the piles of paper and spending hours sifting through them looking for important information. So you start with one pile, but before long, you come across some papers you don't feel like acting on or can't decide what to do with

One effective way of keeping papers visible is to use a vertical receptacle so that the papers stand up and you can flip through them fast.

for one reason or another. You put down that pile and start with another. The same thing happens.

Before you know it, three hours have passed and the only thing that has changed is the clock, which said 9:00 when you began and now says 12:00. You feel even more discouraged.

For now, ignore all those old piles. The time will come to deal with them, and you will become more skilled at doing it as you practice.

To Sort Short

Begin by putting today's mail, or whatever pile of papers you wish to organize, into your To-Sort Tray. Don't feel that this has to be a tray. A box, bin, basket, shelf, or just a designated spot on a desk or table will do nicely.

The key to remember is that the To-Sort Tray is a temporary spot for papers that you have not yet identified (sorted out), i.e., the mail you grabbed out of the box, papers given to you by other family members, papers picked up at a meeting or taken out of your own briefcase. In fact, you may need to have a tray on each floor to transport papers from purses, pockets, drawers, etc., to your desk for action.

"Well," you say, "there's nothing so special about that. I already have sixteen to-sort piles all around the house. There's even one in the bathroom! And I've got half a dozen on my desk at work. I'm very good at to-sort piles!" Here's where the discipline comes in. To make the To-Sort Tray work for you, you must learn to:

- **Sort short.** Be prepared to keep your papers in this temporary resting spot a short time only.
- **Use your to-sort spot consistently.**

The trick to changing your habits and making this system work is to do the sorting frequently, before the next pile begins. Your To-Sort Tray is the place for papers to rest until you can get to the sorting. If it is becoming a permanent home, you are not sorting often enough.

CHAPTER 6

Master the Art of Wastebasketry

When you're ready to attack the contents of your To-Sort Tray, the first objective is to eliminate any paper that's easily identifiable as unnecessary. It is not accidental that the wastebasket comes at the top end of the paper-management system; if you can learn to toss unneeded paper as soon as you encounter it, you're on your way toward effective paper management.

My experience has shown that we never use roughly 80% of the paper we collect. Years of dealing with people and their paper have convinced me that the ability to achieve goals is directly related to a willingness to use the wastebasket. And there's no doubt that, in the long run, your stress level will decrease as the amount of paper in your wastebasket increases. Please note: For the purposes of this discussion, wastebasket also means recycling bin or paper shredder.

When I first began my career as a professional organizing consultant, I had nightmares that distressed or irate clients would call after I had helped them eliminate some of the paper in their life. In twenty-plus years, it has never happened. There are very few pieces of paper we can't live without, and most of us would improve the quality of our lives significantly if we eliminated a lot more.

Enough Is Enough

But even before we deal with effective use of the wastebasket, let's consider ways to reduce the amount of paper that gets to you in the first place. Just about every day a new torrent of paper enters our lives—newspapers, magazines, mail-order catalogs, bills, requests for donations, canceled checks, memos, reminders, invitations, school papers, personal correspondence, and probably the most frustrating of all, "junk mail."

Whenever you place an order from a catalog or request information about a product or a service, you can be certain your name will be passed on to other companies. Even the telephone-directory companies sell mailing lists. If you have difficulty throwing away "junk mail" or would prefer not to have to, explore ways to remove yourself from mailing lists. The box on page 35 suggests several ways to do so.

Unfortunately, there is no guaranteed way to eliminate all you don't want, but the above steps will be a start. In the meantime, keep practicing your Art of Wastebasketry skills!

The overwhelming majority of papers you receive in the mail will eventually end up in the garbage anyway. The issue is whether or not they will first be allowed to collect dust in your home.

"Do I Really Need This?"

Now back to the wastebasket. Each day brings a world of opportunities—frequent-flier bonus offers, entertainment and educational opportunities, information about new services and stores, magazines with articles you want to save (travel, hobbies, recipes, etc.). But to take advantage of any of these opportunities, you need to be able to retrieve the appropriate information at the right moment.

Uncontrolled information is a burden, not a resource. Piles of magazines with interesting, informative articles soon become dust collectors that take up space and create guilt. A collection of information on health and exercise equipment soon takes up as much space as an exercise bicycle, but does nothing to help you increase stamina or lose weight.

Get tough. Take each piece of paper and analyze it by asking each of the following questions. This may be difficult at first, but after a while you'll run through the questions automatically, and you will actually begin to enjoy throwing papers out. I play a game with myself to see how many papers I can get in the wastebasket before they even make it to the desk. Here are the questions to ask yourself:

DID I ASK FOR THIS INFORMATION? Much of the information we receive is sent to us automatically because of computer mailing lists, or friends or relatives send us articles they think might interest us.

IS THIS THE ONLY PLACE THE INFORMATION IS AVAILABLE? Is it in a book you already have? For example, information about taking care of geraniums might also be in a book you have on plant care. Would it be easy enough to get the information from the library or a colleague if you decided you really needed it? Do you have an audio or video tape or CD or DVD with the same information? Is the information stored in your computer or on a disk? Many businesses such as banks, credit-card companies, utility companies and frequent-flier programs offer incentives for you to check your balance online or receive your statements via e-mail. Here is a piece of junk mail to pay attention to—consider using the online options, collect bonus points and eliminate mailings from that company forever.

WOULD IT BE DIFFICULT TO REPLACE? I am a member of several non-profit boards. Recently I looked at file after file of meeting minutes and decided that I did not need to keep these, since we have a board secretary whose job it is to keep records. If I ever needed to refer to a file, all I have to do is access the board files.

IS THE INFORMATION RECENT ENOUGH TO BE USEFUL? A two-year-old restaurant directory is of limited value. Addresses in a mailing list for a party given four years ago will be highly inaccurate.

CAN I IDENTIFY THE SPECIFIC CIRCUMSTANCES WHEN I WOULD WANT THIS INFORMATION? "Just in case" is not a sufficient answer. If you cannot identify how you would use the information, it is unlikely that you would remember that you have it or be able to find it. Keep in mind Hemphill's Principle: "If you don't know you have it, or you can't find it, it is of no value to you."

ARE THERE ANY TAX OR LEGAL IMPLICATIONS? Would the IRS request this information in the event of an audit? Is there any possibility of a lawsuit related to this information?

If the answer to all the above questions is "No," but you're still reluctant to throw that piece of paper away, then ask this question:

WHAT'S THE WORST THING THAT COULD HAPPEN IF I DIDN'T HAVE THIS PIECE OF PAPER? If you can live with the consequences, toss the paper immediately!

Remember: Always open your mail next to the "circular file"—the wastebasket. It will make it easier for you to toss things out, and throwing the paper on the floor beside you would only make extra work. Always ask yourself, "Do I really need or want to keep this?"

In the first few months of my career as an organizing consultant, I was hired by a highly respected professional to organize her condominium. When I opened her door, I was shocked to see piles of paper, several feet deep, surrounded by small piles of paper that were obviously multiple attempts to "get organized." Before long, she confessed that she had finally succumbed to calling me because, when the condominium association sent someone to do a routine spraying for insects he reported that her home had been ransacked! Since that incident, I have met dozens of people who have not had guests in their homes for years because they were too embarrassed by their piles of paper. Life is too short to live it embarrassed!

WAYS TO ELIMINATE UNWANTED MAIL

- **The Mail Preference Service** (MPS) is a consumer service sponsored by The Direct Marketing Association that helps you get your name removed from mailing lists. You can access information by visiting the Web site at www.dma.org and clicking on consumer assistance. All instructions and forms are on the site. Or you can call them at 212-768-7277 (New York) or 202-955-5030 (Washington, D.C.).

- **Many applications and order forms** contain a box you can check if you do not wish to be put on the other mailing lists. Check the box! Or use a preprinted label or rubber stamp that reads: "Do not use, sell, rent or transfer my name on any mailing lists."

- **Create a form letter** and send to all the organizations whose mailings you'd rather not receive at home or at the office and ask them to remove your name from their databases.

- **Be very careful about giving out your name,** business address, and phone number. If you do, request that your name be placed on an "in-house list" only. Lately I have noticed that local stores will ask for my mailing information or phone number when routinely ringing up an order. If you'd rather not, say so. The reaction is always "Oh, OK." It is not necessary to provide all this information to make a purchase. The stores are just building their mailing list.

- **Avoid the post office's change-of-address system** when moving. Unless you want the post office selling your name over and over again, send your own postcards.

- **If you return warranty cards,** add a note saying that you want your name kept private. You are covered by the manufacturer's warranty whether you return the card or not. The only reason to return a card is to find out about product recalls. Provide only your name, address and product's serial number. If you check that you are interested in computers, you are sure to hear from computer companies.

- **Don't enter sweepstakes.**

- **For even more ideas to stop unwanted mail,** send $3 to Good Advice Press, Elizaville, NY 12523 and request a copy of *Stop Junk Mail Forever.*

Recycling

I would be remiss if I did not discuss the issue of recycling in effective paper-management techniques. There are a variety of recycling opportunities, from recycling individual types of paper, such as newspapers and white paper, to recycling magazines by giving them to organizations or individuals that will put them to good use. You can use your Zip code to find local recycling options for computers and other materials. Check out www.1800cleanup.org.

One client of mine had stacks of beautiful art-related magazines in her office. She admitted that she never read them but could not bear to part with them—until we found a group that shipped magazines to libraries in Poland. It was quite a sight seeing her red Jaguar stuffed with magazines with just enough room for the driver!

The Issue of Privacy

For some people, one of the stumbling blocks to getting rid of paper is the issue of privacy. Unfortunately, it is becoming a bigger issue as we move further down the electronic information highway. Fortunately, the solution is getting simpler. Personal shredders have become affordable, and the results of your personal destruction can even be recycled for packing material, cat litter or confetti.

Your Calendar

The purpose of many of those pieces of paper you collect is to remind you to do something. As a result, you can eliminate a considerable amount of paper from your desks, dresser tops, mirrors, purses and wallets simply by effectively using an important action tool: your calendar. The key here is to get into the habit of extrapolating the information you need from the paper, entering it on your calendar, and then throwing out the pieces of paper or, if you really think you'll need the information in the future, filing it away in your rotary phone file or in your Reference File.

Calendars used in the way I'll describe in this chapter not only help eliminate paper clutter, but also the mind clutter that comes from having to remember too many details and dates at one time.

Your Master Calendar

It wasn't so long ago that keeping track of our schedules was fairly simple. Husbands went off to work and kept their business schedules at the office. If an after-work business appointment needed to be made, the husband—ideally—called home first to be sure there was no conflict. Wives kept the home running smoothly, keeping track of the kids' schedules and making sure social engagements weren't missed.

Life is not so simple anymore. Now men are much more concerned with being involved fathers, too. They want to know when the next soccer game will be, what

You can use your calendar not only as an appointment calendar but also as a tool for effective follow-up.

time their child's play will begin, and when the child has no school and will have to go to the office with dad.

And of course it's not just the husband who's out in the work force. More and more families have both partners off to work each day—and both of them must keep their own schedules while trying not to create conflicts with their spouse's. Scheduling becomes even more complicated for people who have divorced and have children.

The most effective paper managers I know have a Master Calendar on which all commitments—business and personal for all family members—are recorded. If you're fortunate enough that you can keep your business life separate from your personal life, you can keep one calendar at the office and another at home. But if you're like most people, you'll need the combined business/personal Master Calendar, which you might keep at home or in the office—or perhaps it will be a portable one that you carry with you in a briefcase, your suit-jacket pocket or purse. Or perhaps you prefer to keep track of appointments on a laptop computer or a personal information manager or personal digital assistant (see page 45).

You may ask, "How important is it to carry my calendar with me?" If you do not already carry one, for several days try keeping track of how many times you would have referred to your calendar if you had it with you.

In addition to your Master Calendar, you may need other calendars for specific functions. For example, because I do a lot of consulting around the country, I have a calendar on the wall of my office that shows my travel schedule. But don't get caught in the trap of having more calendars than you can manage. The key to the success of more than one calendar is to identify clearly the specific purpose of each.

Coordinating Your Schedule

A major complication of calendars is coordination. Keeping associates and family members informed of changing commitments is an ongoing challenge.

Most families find it crucial to hang a calendar in some strategic location in their house to communicate information that affects the family, such as travel and sports schedules, family celebrations or doctors' appointments. Many people put their calendar on the refrigerator, since everyone ends up there sooner or later.

Put Your Calendar to Work

Here's how it works. Let's say you receive a meeting notice in the mail. Frequently you can enter the information—time, place, telephone number—directly into your calendar and throw the notice away. If there is more essential information on the notice than what will fit in your calendar, such as an agenda, directions, etc., you can note the name of the meeting in your calendar and put the notice itself into a Pending Action File (see Chapter 11). Put a "P" beside the notation in your calendar, so you will know that further information can be found in your Pending file. (For some other handy abbreviations I use on my calendar, see the list in the box at right.)

Suppose you read in the newspaper about a concert you would like to attend, if you get home from work in time and if there are no other family obligations. Put the date of the concert in your calendar—in pencil—both on the day by which you must buy tickets and on the day of the event. If you simply leave the notice on your desk so that you won't forget, you are likely to handle that piece of paper dozens of times and still not attend the concert.

If you've written a letter or memo to someone and you need to get a reply in two weeks, make a note to yourself in your calendar, "Heard from John?"

You can see that you can use your calendar not only as an appointment calendar but also as a tool for effective follow-up. If there are specific materials you want to remember to check when you follow up, make a note of that directly in your calendar.

FOR YOUR CALENDAR

The following are some abbreviations I use on my calendar to help remind me of what I'm to do. As you think of others that you could use, add them to the list.

C	Call
CE	Calls Expected (they will call me)
D	See Discuss Action File
P	See Pending Action File
LM	Left Message
NA	No Answer

USE ONLY WHAT YOU NEED

I once sat next to a woman on an airplane who was holding a beautiful leather-bound calendar with her name inscribed in gold. She suddenly let out a big sigh. "Is something wrong?" I asked. "I must be hopeless," she said. "My husband bought me this beautiful calendar, and I don't even know what to do with it." We spent the next hour assessing her needs—and eliminated half of the pages in the calendar.

Make an Appointment With Yourself

In my experience, the people who are most successful in managing their time and accomplishing their goals are those who make appointments with themselves. I've found the most effective way to organize my life is to sit down every Sunday evening and identify the most important things I want to accomplish in the week ahead and note them in my calendar. Whenever you choose to do it, do it regularly. And when you do, determine the specific tasks you want to accomplish in various areas of your life. For example, if you are trying to improve your exercise habits, decide what days of the week you will exercise, and where and how you will do it.

You can also use your calendar to make notes to remind yourself to check on specific issues. For example, you're at a meeting and you agree to complete a certain task. Make a quick calculation about when you need to begin work and write a note to yourself on your calendar, if you carry it with you. If you don't, put an asterisk beside your note to remind you to enter the information in your calendar when you return home or to the office. In this way you avoid creating additional pieces of paper and you will be reminded at exactly the right time.

If there is a specific task you need to do (for example, clean out your file drawer or spend some time on your to-read pile—see Chapter 15), make an appointment with yourself, just as you would with someone else.

Some people are hesitant to use this approach because they don't want to become too compulsive. They shudder to think of themselves talking to a friend and having to say, "I need to go now. I have to catch up on my reading." I'm not suggesting such inflexibility!

Using your calendar as a time-management tool helps you to be realistic about your time. If you have blocked out an hour to write the minutes from your last committee meeting and you decide you would rather do something else or you have to take your child to the doctor, you can realistically decide on your options for that given day. You can write the minutes while you are waiting at the doctor's office or block out time later in the week. But do make sure you keep your commitment to yourself in one way or another.

Choose Your Calendar Wisely

There are hundreds of calendars on the market and choosing one can be frustrating. Many calendars are so complicated that you have to take a training course to learn how to use them. Keep in mind that just because a company includes something in a calendar or planner doesn't mean you have to use it.

You should consider a few things when you select your calendar. If you use your calendar as I've described, you need to select one with plenty of writing space. Of course, this will mean a larger calendar, and, if you don't regularly carry a purse or a briefcase, you may feel this is not practical and you will have to make adjustments. One alternative to give you additional writing space is to use removable notes, which can be affixed to your calendar and removed when you have completed the tasks.

Format is the second factor to consider. Do you need to see each day, the month, the whole year, or a combination?

My experience is that the best paper managers use a combination—a weekly calendar for short-term planning, and a monthly or yearly one for long-term planning, and for recording "non-negotiable" appointments and re-

continued on page 44

✂ A LOOK AT MY CALENDAR

Here's a sample of my favorite paper calendar. I use the yearly section for an overview of what lies ahead (last six months shown below). Abbreviations and short descriptions let me know where I'll be (Boston on the 7th, for example), family schedules (I use a differ- ent color pencil for each family member), and important events (Pat H. birthday on 4th). Appointments, daily to-do's and projects go in the weekly section (left-hand page, shown opposite) under my different roles. Expense notations are on the right-hand page not shown here.

	SUNDAY	MONDAY	TUESDAY	WEDNESDAY	THURSDAY	FRIDAY	SATURDAY
						1 CANADA DAY	2
JUL	3	4 PAT H. INDEPENDENCE DAY	5	6	7 ADIE/CHUCK BOSTON	8	9
	10	11	12 RON -MARIE	13	14 BETTY	15	16
	17	18	19 ABERNATHY	20	21	22 PAM	23
	24	25 BOOK FAIR	26	27	28	29	30 BOBBIE
AUG	31	1	2 WINSTON-SALEM	3	4 — ASHEVILLE	5	6 NAPO BOARD
	7	8	9 — VACATION	10	11	12	13
	14 JOHA-21	15	16 — VACATION	17	18	19	20
	21	22 — ATLANTA	23	24	25	26	27 DUKE
	28	29 HAIRCUT	30	31	1	2	3
SEP	4	5 ABOR DAY	6 ROSH HASHANAH	7 HEIDI TO SCHOOL	8	9 CSA	10 AT/DRILL
	11 AT/DRILL	12 DUKE	13 AT/BH ANNIVERSARY	14	15 YOM KIPP.	16	17
	18	19	20	21 NATION'S BANK NCSU	22 ASJA — ASHEVILLE	23	24
	25	26	27 HOWARD COUNTY	28	29 WASH DC	30	1
OCT	2	3 RADIO TOUR —	4 GET ORGANIZED	5	6 WEEK —	7	8
	9	10 CHARLOTTE COLUMBUS DAY OBV THANKSGIVING DAY (CAN)	11	12 COLUMBUS DAY	13 BEN - 21 HEIDI —	14	15 STANTON
	16	17	18 NAPO	19	20 NCSU	21	22
	23	24	25	26	27	28	29
NOV	30	31 HALLOWEEN	1 ELECTION DAY	2	3	4 — NAPO RETREAT —	5
	6	7	8	9 ASTD	10	11 VETERAN'S DAY	12
	13	14	15 WASH DC	16	17	18	19
	20	21 NAPO-DC	22	23 HEIDI	24 THANKSGIVING DAY	25	26
DEC	27	28 CHANUKAH BEGINS	29	30	1	2	3
	4	5 — FT. LAUDERDALE	6	7	8	9	10
	11	13	13	14	15	16	17
	18	19	20	21 HEIDI —	22	23	24
	25 CHRISTMAS DAY	26	27	28	29	30	31

YEARLY PLANNER

PLANNING FOR THE WEEK OF: *AUGUST 22*

WEEKLY LISTS OF ACTIVITIES BY CATEGORIES

H & A	SPEAKER/WRITER	NAPO	FAMILY
TRIANGLE AD	HEARD FROM TIME? (CE)	CALL CHRIS (C)	CHAIRS/BED TO
NCSU	NCSU SEMINAR PLAN	LETTER TO ARIZ	CHURCH 878-9335
BROCHURE COPY	TAMING CORRECTIONS	BY-LAW REVISION	HEARD FROM MARGARET?
VIDEO FEEDBACK?		CONTRACT	MORTGAGE APPLICATION
FLYERS RE DUKE		NEW ADDRESS	CALL LANDSCAPER
			RSVP - SK WEDDING (P)

DAILY THINGS-TO-DO

MONDAY 22	TUESDAY 23	WEDNESDAY 24	THURSDAY 25
TAMING CORRECTIONS	MARY HIGGINS	CALL RENETTE	CALL CHICAGO (P)
BOB BAILEY	924-5267	834-3722 (W)	
700-902-8202	ALEX - GOING TONIGHT?	CHRISTY-NAPO? (CE)	
MOLLY GLANDER	JAN SWANSON	600-322-9753	
CALL RON FALKIN	800-790-1342		
REMAX 242-3100	INFO TO STAPLES		
CALL GREER –			
SEE 8/11			
CALL SUSANNE			

APPOINTMENTS

DADDY'S BIRTHDAY	7	7	7 BREAKFAST/CLUB - K.C.
8	8	8	8
9	9 NATION'S BANK	9	9 NCSU - DELIVER ART
10	10 ROD - 829-6633	10	10
11	11	11	11
12	12	12	12 MOLLY / KAY
1	1	1	1 RE COVEY
2 HAIRCUT	2	2	2
3	3 30 NCSU - PAM SMITH	3	3
4	4 2190 BERLIN Rd.	4	4
5	5 501-3470	5	5
6	6	6	6
7 WRITING	7	7	7
8	8 ENNIS	8	8
9	9	9	9

(Wednesday diagonal note: SUCCESS SEMINAR GREENSBORO HILTON)

PLANNER PAD®

P=Pending   **LM**=Left message   **CE**=Calls expected   **D**=Discuss   **C**=Call minders, such as travel schedule and children's birthdays.

I don't think I've ever met anyone who has found the perfect calendar. I hear comments such as, "This calendar is great, except it's too big," or "There isn't enough writing space." With your calendar, as with many things in life, you can have anything you want, but not everything you want. Many of my clients combine the best parts of two calendars.

I use an 8½" x 11" Planner Pad. There's a two-page yearly calendar in the front that gives me room for long-range planning and provides just enough space for me to write key words such as a client's name, the city where I'll be, my son's birthday, etc.

The rest of the Planner Pad is made up of a series of two facing pages for each week. The pages are divided into three sections. The bottom third is for specific appointments Monday through Sunday from 7:00 A.M. to 9:00 P.M. (I like the long hours, since I can easily include breakfast and dinner appointments.) The middle third I use for my daily to-do lists—phone calls, reminders, etc. The top third is what I use on Sunday evening to identify my priorities for the week in each of the areas of my life. There's room at the bottom of the right-hand page for me to note deductible expenses. This format is particularly pleasing when Uncle Sam calls!

To increase usability, I purchase stick-on tabs to identify specific months of the year, and peel-off pockets for the front and back covers to hold receipts, business cards, etc. I cut off the corner of the page at the end of the week. The back of the Planner Pad has pages that I use for my to-do lists (more about that in Chapter 8).

For a look at how my Planner Pad calendar works, see pages 42 and 43. (To receive free Planner Pad information, visit www.plannerpads.com or call 402-592-0676 and mention this book.)

Electronic Calendar Keeping

The increase in the availability and capability of electronic calendars is mindboggling. If you are totally comfortable with electronics, you may find a portable electronic calendar that you can carry in your pocket or briefcase a perfect solution.

The PIM (Personal Information Manager) products have a growing number of options, including a calendar, an address book, note-taking modules, alarms, task managers, phone logs, e-mail and even fax capability—and they're getting easier and easier for nontechnical people to use. In addition, many of them can also be synchronized with your desktop computer so that you can take information from the computer and put it on your PIM, and vice versa.

Many people have traded their paper calendars and address books for a personal digital assistant, or PDA, a remarkable, tiny, fully functional computer that you can hold in one hand. And unlike those paper organizers, a PDA can hold your downloaded e-mail and play music. PDAs are one of the fastest-selling consumer devices in history. According to www.howstuffworks.com, more than nine million hand-held computers have been sold, the vast majority of them from one company, Palm Computing. But other companies are breaking into the market, meaning that you have more features to choose from and decisions to make before you buy a PDA.

Still, many of my clients find that a hard-copy calendar works just fine. One lawyer I know carries a pocket calendar in which he notes all appointments that will occur outside his office, such as meal or evening and out-of-town appointments. He tracks all other appointments on his computer calendar.

The bottom line is that what you decide to do is not nearly as important as doing it consistently!

Your To-Do Lists

Does this sound familiar? You're trying to go to sleep and you suddenly remember, "Oh, I never called my insurance company to take John off the automobile policy!" Or, while driving home from the hardware store, you realize you forgot to get that extra house key the cleaning service has needed for the past month.

Experiences like these are the basis for the piles of notes scratched on the back of empty envelopes, on the corner of the newspaper or on any scrap of paper that happens to be lying around. Many of the pieces of paper in the piles around the house and scattered over our desks at work are there to serve as reminders of things we want to do at some point in the future—tomorrow, next week, or maybe not until we retire!

To Do or Not To Do

The purpose of the to-do list—another "Action," too—is to provide a consistent place to compile notes to yourself, and in so doing to eliminate many pieces of paper from your life. One of my clients called such a list "a depository for your thoughts."

Some people decry the whole idea, feeling that if they write something down they might absolve themselves from doing it. In fact, making a list of the things you need to do is the first step to developing a goal-setting technique that is essential for effective life management.

One of the major joys of a to-do list is crossing items off when they are completed. I put a check by the items

I have completed on the daily to-do list. I always check the list from the two previous days. If I didn't get it done in three days, I try to figure out why, and what I can do about it. One client admitted that periodically he makes lists of things he's already done just so he can cross them off! In fact, I have discovered that if you spend a day dealing with crisis after crisis, and nothing on your to-do list gets checked off, it can be an excellent learning process to make a list of what you actually did. Then you can analyze the list to see if there was something you could have done to prevent the crisis.

What To Do First

Success in life can come from doing things right—but first we have to make sure we are doing the right things. One of the ongoing issues for everyone I know—and for me as well—is deciding what to do first. Let me suggest an exercise to assist you in improving your ability to decide what is the right thing to do first.

Take a look at your life over the last several months. What results have you had during this time period that you would like to repeat? When I completed the exercise, I recognized that one of my most fulfilling activities was speaking to large audiences. When I analyzed how I got those opportunities, I could identify actions I needed to take to ensure that I could multiply my opportunities—namely, spending time developing relationships with meeting planners who have the ability to hire speakers for large audiences.

Or to put it another way, what's one thing you could do that would bring about something you really want? When I asked myself that question, my answer was, "I want to be physically fit." My challenge then was identifying what specific actions I needed to take to make that happen.

How To Do It

There are probably as many kinds of to-do lists as there are list makers. Keep in mind that some to-do's are tasks that need to be done at a specific time, such as "mail a birthday card to Aunt Sally," while others are things you want to do but have not yet determined when you can do them, such as "buy birthday cards." Chances of completing the to-do's with specific dates improve if you enter them in your calendar (see Chapter 7). The rest of the to-do's go on a master to-do list, which may or may not be in your calendar.

People have different criteria for what they include in their list and how they include it. Some just use key words, like "Call Jerry," but what if you look at the list and you can't remember why? Others add notes about the topic to be discussed and the phone number so they don't have to look it up when it's time to call. There is also the ongoing debate over whether to separate at-home to-do's from work to-do's. Some people keep a running list, and when it gets messy or full they start over.

The more information you want to put on your to-do list, the more cluttered your list will become, and the less helpful it will be. One solution for this is to devise coded symbols to record progress on a task. You can use many of the same ones you use on your calendar (see page 39).

There are also numerous software programs and electronic gadgets for managing to-do lists along with your calendar. These include Personal Information Managers such as *ACT!*, *Goldmine* or *Outlook* and Personal Digital Assistants such as Palm Pilots. These devices are the perfect answer for some people and nothing but frustration for others. The decision about how to do your to-do list will depend on how and when you use it. You may, in fact, have more than one list.

Like With Like

One basic principle when organizing anything is to put like items together. Some people apply this principle to organizing lists. Put items on a to-do list together based on the kind of activity required. For example, group together all phone calls, all letters to write and all errands to run. When you're running errands, you

continued on page 52

FOR YOUR TO-DO LIST

Your to-do list can be divided into lots of categories, depending on your specific needs. The following are some possibilities. Check off those you want to use. If you think of others not described here, use the space provided to write them down. Keep in mind that you need to determine not only the categories of your to-do list, but also where it should be located physically.

Birthdays. Most of us have good intentions about remembering those special days of family members and friends. You can create a special section in your to-do book. This makes it easy to translate onto your calendar the days you need to mail the cards or to purchase the cards you need when you are running errands.

Books, Tapes and CDs. Eliminate those torn, yellowed newspaper articles about books you have been meaning to purchase. List books you want to borrow from the library. (If the book is checked out when you go to check it out, note the Dewey Decimal number when you look it up the first time, so you don't have to look it up again.) You can also list books or tapes you have loaned to friends.

Discuss. This category provides a place to accumulate information you want to discuss with a particular person. Use one section for each person in your life with whom you interact frequently: boss, assistant, child, spouse, committee chair, etc.

Use another section to list questions you want to ask your doctor at your next appointment, another to list the items that you need to discuss with your mechanic the next time you take your car to the garage, or another to list concerns you want to raise at the next parent-teacher conference at school.

Errands. Have you ever gone past the appliance-repair shop wishing you had the style number of the vacuum bags so you could pick them up on the way home instead of making an extra trip? This section will save you many miles of errand running. (The To-Do Book also has a pocket to put such items as dry cleaning receipts, etc., so you'll be sure to have them when you need them.)

Group errands together according to geographical area or type of store. Most people keep their grocery list in the kitchen, but if you happen to be at work when you think of something that needs to go on the list, this is a great place to put it. Then when you are ready to go grocery shopping, you can combine both lists.

Gifts. Remember that perfect gift you found hidden in a closet after you spent two hours looking for a housewarming gift for your new neighbor? Here's a place to list the gifts you have on hand—and where they are located if you are afraid you will forget. (Be careful, of course, about spoiling a surprise by listing gifts for the family.) You can also make a note when you overhear your father saying he really would like to have a good pair of binoculars. You might even make a list of gift ideas for yourself, in case your kids ever ask. (I post mine prominently on the refrigerator just before Christmas and my birthday!)

Goals. Research shows that fewer than 3% of the U.S. population put their goals in writing. It also shows that having written goals is high on the priority list of high achievers. Whether you are making New Year's resolutions or designing a business plan, this section provides a convenient place to keep track of your goals and your progress. Then it will be easy to check periodically to see if your life activities reflect what you said you wanted to do. (Goals qualifies as one of those categories you don't need to carry with you all the time.)

Letters. We all mean to write more letters than we ever put in the mail. One letter a week, and you've kept in touch with 52 people. This section also could be divided into personal and business. Do whatever you can to make it easy to keep in touch— take advantage of hotel stationery, buy postcards when you travel, carry stationery with you or use e-mail.

Numbers. Frequently the papers in our piles contain numbers we need to remember. Be cautious about listing numbers you don't want other people to know, such as access codes to the ATM machine, the long-distance service, or your security system. However, having quick access to insurance-policy numbers, social security numbers for other family members, club membership or frequent-traveler numbers, as well as refill numbers or clothing sizes can be helpful.

Phone Calls. List the names of people you need to call, with the phone number beside them to speed up the process. You may find it helpful to use one section for personal calls and another for business. If you need to make a phone call at a specific time, use your calendar, not your to-do list (or use both—as a security measure).

Projects. Planning to redecorate your living room or give a Super Bowl party? Here is a place to collect all the ideas you have. (One client puts a small sample of her wallpaper, paint, fabric swatches etc. in her to-do book.) Then as you begin the project, you can enter the various steps into your calendar as they need to be completed.

Restaurants. Here you can record names of restaurants you would like to try, with addresses, phone numbers and business hours. You may even want to add the name of the maitre d'. Group the restaurants together by geographical area. Then if you are meeting a friend or client downtown, you can easily check your list to see which restaurant would be most suitable

continued on page 52

FOR YOUR TO-DO LIST (continued)

and convenient.

This system will also eliminate all the pieces of paper with restaurant reviews you have been saving. And it's fun when a guest comes to town and says, "Let's go out tonight." It will take you no time to choose your restaurant.

Thoughts. How many times have you read a quote that intrigued you or had a brainstorm about how to solve a particular problem and said to yourself, "I'll have to give that some thought?" Write those ideas down. If you carry them with you and find yourself caught in rush-hour traffic or waiting in the banker's office, you can decide what step you need to take next.

Travel. A to-do book is a terrific place to put a standard packing list for travel. Then each time you plan a trip to a new city, create a special page. Make notes about particular things you want to take with you, people you want to see or places you want to go, or information about car rentals, hotel reservations, etc. Finally, make a Before-Trip Checklist as a reminder about those last-minute to-do's, such as checking the thermostat, turning off the coffee pot, making arrangements to feed the cat, and stopping the newspaper. Some frequent travelers make an After-Trip Checklist to remind themselves of something they want to do differently on the next trip.

won't be distracted by a list of phone calls you need to make. Or if you are trying to make a series of phone calls, you won't be bothered by a note to buy blank tapes.

Some people just keep a running list. I keep some to-do categories in the calendar I carry with me, such as Errands and Numbers, while other categories stay in the loose-leaf book at home and another book at the office. You can use temporary labels, notations in your calendar or index cards in your pocket to remind yourself to enter a to-do on a list that is not accessible at the time.

Also consider frequency of use when you decide where to list your to-do's. Let me explain. One time I was discussing the subject of getting organized with a gentleman sitting next to me on an airplane. He commented, "Some of the things on my to-do list have been there for years." By the tone of his voice it was evident that he expected my disapproval—which he didn't get! There are certainly things I want to do that I've been thinking about for years—such as taking a trip to Alaska and writing a family history. I have an Annual To-Do List—ideas for major projects that I consider once a year. I keep that list in my computer. There's no point carrying it around with me. So if you decide to have more than one to-do list, consider keeping them where you will most likely use them.

To Carry or Not to Carry?

Should you carry your to-do list with you? The proponents of the to-do list on a yellow legal pad might find this difficult. Some people use a small spiral notebook or even index cards they can stick in their pocket. Adhesive notes make a handy to-do list when you need to put a reminder in a can't-miss-it place—such as in the car, on the outside of your briefcase or purse or on the bathroom mirror.

> **CAUTION!**
>
> Clean out your to-do book from time to time. If lists become overwhelming, ask yourself these questions:
> - Is there someone who could help me get this done?
> - Is there a way to simplify this task?
> - Would it matter if I put it off for _____ days/weeks/months?
> - What's the worst possible thing that would happen if I didn't do this?

But to really get a firm hold on the paper in your life, I strongly recommend that you create some system to carry to do's with you when appropriate. For people who want to carry their to-do list but don't want to carry their calendar, I created The To Do Book, a 3$\frac{1}{2}$" x 6$\frac{1}{2}$" loose-leaf notebook that has a pocket inside the front and back covers. The loose-leaf format makes it easy to add and delete pages. I divided the notebook into sections, using the categories described on pages 50-52. (For information about ordering The To Do Book, call 800-427-0237.)

My portable to-do list can be a big time saver. For example, if I'm stuck in a traffic jam or waiting in a doctor's office, I use the time to plan projects, make my to-do list for the next day, or write a quick thank-you note. (I always carry one or two pieces of note stationery in the notebook's back pocket). If I'm near a shopping center and I have an extra ten minutes before I need to get to an appointment, I can check the Errands section in my list and find one or two things I can accomplish in that time.

Remember I said that one of the objectives of this paper-management system is to eliminate unnecessary pieces of paper. Try just these first four aspects of the system—the To-Sort Tray, the wastebasket, the calendar, and the to-do list—and see how much paper you can toss. The next three chapters offer help in determining what to do with those pieces of paper you have to keep.

CHAPTER 9

Your Names and Numbers

S ome of the most crucial pieces of information you need to have ready access to are names and numbers.

If you suddenly decide to take a trip to San Francisco, it's unlikely that you will even re-member that the telephone number of your favorite cousin, who lives there, is in one of the letters buried on the desk. Even if you do remember, what are the chances you will have the time to look for it? Remember Hemphill's Principle: "If you don't know you have it, or you can't find it, it is of no value to you!" Many of the pieces of paper floating around our homes are there be-cause they have an important telephone number written or printed on them—or because we are afraid the num-ber might become important to us.

Residential and Commercial Listings

In our personal lives telephone numbers can be divided into two basic categories: relatives and close friends with whom we always want to stay in contact regardless of where we live; and neighbors, services, stores, schools, organizations or government agencies with whom we will no longer have contact if we move.

In other words, each of us needs a personal residen-tial phone list and a personal commercial list. For many people who move frequently, it is essential to separate those two categories so when they do move it is easy to tear out the Minneapolis listings and start Denver.

The first step in designing a good system for addresses and telephone numbers is to determine whether you wish to separate your residential and your commercial listings into different systems or use one system. Your choice will be influenced to some extent by the volume of information you want to keep. If you have a career, a family, an active community life or travel frequently, you may need more than one.

Choose Your System

The next step is to decide on the system of listing you will use. Options range from something as simple as a loose-leaf notebook or preprinted telephone and address book to a box of alphabetized index cards—or its far more efficient cousin, a rotary card file such as those made by Rolodex—or a program for your personal computer.

In making your decision, keep in mind how portable your system needs to be or whether you plan duplicate systems for office, home, vacation home or travel. Whatever system you choose, the determining factor in the success of your system is ensuring that you will be able to retrieve the information when you need it.

You'll probably need several phone systems. At home, you should have a complete listing of residential and commercial listings at your work area. If your home has more than one floor or if you have more than one home, you will need additional systems to accommodate those needs, based on what calls you're most likely to make where. For example, I frequently make telephone calls to family members from my bedroom, but nearly always make business-related calls from my office area. (Yes, there will be times when the number you need will be in the wrong place, but remember that organization isn't about perfection, just progress.)

In addition, you should have a small telephone book or use the back part of your portable calendar to record the most frequently used numbers so you have access to the numbers when you're away from home or at the office. If you use a separate small phone book instead of a section of your calendar, you won't have to worry about rewriting the phone information at the end of each year On the other hand, if you are willing to take the time, it's a valuable exercise to purge your portable phone list at the end of each year.

But How Can I Find It?

The major advantage of an electronic system for recording names and numbers is that, because of the search capability available with a computer chip, finding who or what you're looking for is relatively simple. Many programs have a notes section where you can put all kinds of details, such as where you met someone, who introduced you, etc. In some electronic programs, even that section is searchable, which means that the more information you put in, the more ways you can find it.

Electronic address books range from the simple, such

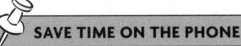

SAVE TIME ON THE PHONE

If you're calling:
1. Group calls when possible.
2. If you call some people frequently and they're hard to reach, ask when the best time is to call.
3. Identify yourself and why you're calling. For example, "Hi, Jerry. This is Pat Roberts. I'm calling to find out what time our homeowner's meeting is on Friday."
4. If your call is complicated, make an agenda and check items off as you discuss them.
5. If you think you won't cover all the issues, prioritize them and start with the most important.
6. At the end of the call, decide when you will call again or what other way

you could get information you need.
7. If you get an answering machine, leave as complete a message as you can. Repeat your number twice, once at the beginning and once at the end of the message. Avoid phone tag by giving options such as when is a good time to reach you or alternate numbers.

When you get a call:
1. Use an answering machine or service to control when you take calls.
2. Use assertive language such as, "What can I do for you?"
3. Be honest! If you don't have time to talk, say so. "I'm sorry, but I can't talk now. When can I call you back?"

as *My Address Book* to the more complex Personal Information Managers such as *ACT!, Goldmine* or *Outlook,*. Most computers come with a default system for home use that is usually more than adequate. Also don't forget that financial-management programs such as *Microsoft Money* or *Quicken* come with an address book, as do e-mail programs such as *Outlook Express.*

EMERGENCY!

There's a serious side to organizing your numbers. If your child becomes ill from drinking a poisonous substance, you won't have time to sort through a pile of papers for the poison-control center's emergency number. Post such numbers by at least one phone on each floor. Include police, fire, poison-control center, work numbers for family members and any neighbor or friend you might call in an emergency.

If you're using a paper system, don't assume that all information should be recorded in the same way. You might list a number under the name of the individual, under the name of the company or organization, by the type of service they perform, and in rare instances, perhaps, even under the name of the person who introduced you.

Sometimes you may wish to record numbers under more than one category. For example, if you are using a card file, you might have one card for Household Repairs on which you list several services. However, you might have a separate card for Pipewrench, Peter—Plumber, or Plumber—Peter Pipewrench. In general, though, the simpler the system is, the more inclined you will be to use it. Ask yourself the question, "What word would I think of if I wanted to contact this person?" Use that answer as your key word for entering the information.

The Rotary Card File

If you've never used a rotary card file, you may be surprised at its usefulness. I have one in the kitchen for emergency and most frequently used numbers. (Rolodex is the most common brand, but Bates, Eldon and Rubbermaid also make them.) If you already have one that you've inherited from someone else or yours isn't working well, start over. Don't make organizing your phone numbers a project for when you have time. Instead, start with a new file and add the numbers from

SAMPLE ROTARY-FILE CARDS

Hemphill, Barbara 919-773-0722
Hemphill Productivity Institute
1464 Garner Station Blvd.
Raleigh, NC 27603
Barbara@ProductiveEnvironment.com
(In this space you could note date/subject of telephone
calls, directions to get the office, etc.)

HOUSE REPAIRS
Plumber—Peter Pipewrench   919-222-4387
Electrician—Henry Wire   919-425-3098
Painter—Betty Brush   919-620-4487

SOCIAL SECURITY NUMBERS
Barbara 50–852–3827
Alfred 312–60–8887
Jenny 508–59–1111
Tommy 508–20–8034

COMBINATION LOCKS
16-3-5 (GYM)
15-1-7 (BICYCLE)

the old one as you use them.

I recommend purchasing a card file that uses 3" x 5" cards. They are large enough to staple or tape business cards directly onto (that way you don't have to copy the information) and provide enough room to give you plenty of writing space. A smaller size rotary file might be just what you need beside the phone in your bedroom.

A standard format will make your rotary system easier to use. Put the key word—an individual's name (last name first), or the name of the organization, business or service—in the upper left-hand corner and the phone number in the upper right, as this is the information you will need most often. Then list the address under the key word. If the person has other phone numbers—a cell phone number, the home number of a business acquaintance or a company's fax number, for example—record these numbers as well. Be sure to note which number is which. Also add any e-mail address.

In addition to name, address and telephone number, the rotary card file can be used for recording other useful information: key people at a business, a simple record of correspondence or telephone exchanges, birthdays, anniversaries, dates of special events.

The file is also an excellent place for tracking your holiday-card list. Make a small chart in the lower right-hand corner with three columns—one for the year, one for sent, and one for received, where you can place check marks. Some people create a separate holiday list, but incorporating it into an existing system frequently means less work and fewer systems to keep updated.

There's no law that says that a rotary card file can be used only for addresses and phone numbers. The file is a perfect place to record bits of information you'd like to have at your fingertips, such as the social security numbers for your family or the combination to your child's bike lock. If you're not worried about security, you could also list all your credit-card numbers with the number to call in case they are lost or stolen. Think of the file as a mini-file for odd bits of information—a place to put information too small for a traditional file folder.

Rotary phone file cards come in a variety of colors that you can use to indicate different categories.

Today's Mail Is Still Tomorrow's Pile

If you have a system that doesn't work—or no system at all—begin one immediately. If you put it aside as a big project, for when things calm down, you are unlikely to accomplish the task. Instead, start the new system with the next phone number you use. In the beginning, use two systems at once. As you pull information out of the old system, incorporate it into the new. Eventually you will combine the two systems into one, or the old one will become so old you will feel comfortable throwing it away.

Your Reference Files

A fter you have eliminated as many pieces of paper as possible by using your wastebasket, calendar and to-do list, and you have established a workable system for finding names and numbers easily, the remaining papers will fall into one of two categories:

ACTION FILES: These files are for those papers that need your attention immediately or at some point in the near future (as opposed to the "someday" projects). The next chapter explains how to set up an efficient Action File system.

REFERENCE FILES: Reference Files are for information you know you will—or think you might—need at some point in the future. Some of this information can be filed in your rotary phone file or phone book; suggestions for doing so are in Chapter 9. After reading Chapter 22 on using the computer to deal with paper, you may also find that some reference papers will be replaced by a good Web site or computer file.

Taken together, the system is particularly effective if you keep two points in mind:
- **A Reference File can become an Action File or vice versa**. For example, a Reference File called Entertaining can become an Action File if you are planning a party. When the party is over, look through the contents of the file, discard material you won't need again, and return the remaining material to your Reference Files.

(This is an important step that many people omit!) Be sure to take a few minutes to throw out any excess papers at this point, instead of saying, "I've got to clean that file out someday." It is much quicker and easier to do while the information is fresh in your mind.

- **You can have an Action File and a Reference File with the same or similar file headings.** For example, you might have a Reference File entitled Community Association for papers you need to keep but which don't require action, and an Action File entitled Community Association—Dues Campaign for a current project.

The reason to create Reference Files is not just to be able to put papers away but it's also to be able to find them again. Let's think of it as creating a Finding System. Research shows that 80% of the papers in most files are never used. So before you even begin to think about where you should file any piece of paper, think seriously about whether you should file it at all.

If you have a filing system that isn't working or if you inherited someone else's system, read this chapter and start over. Don't try to fix the existing files. Instead, incorporate the information from the old system into the new system as you need it.

Using Your Computer for Tracking Files

If you're one of the many people who dislikes making file labels and deciding which two or three words to put on the file tab, consider using *Kiplinger's Taming the Paper Tiger* software. This program takes advantage of the computer's capability to search a large volume of information in a short time—in any order.

Think about it. A good deal of the time you spend filing is really spent determining what files need to be grouped together: Should you take out all the files that are related to taxes and put them in a special category called Financial? What should you call a particular file—

car, automobile or Ford? With the software, you can automatically cross-reference your files with as many words or phrases as you like, easily share information with others, identify a specific date when you want to review a file and, most importantly, find what you're looking for in seconds.

In addition, the software generates file labels and reports you can use to find files when you don't have access to your computer, or to make cleaning your files easier. It can also be used to keep track of items around your home, such as audio and video tapes and CDs. For more information, call 800-427-0237 or go onlne at www.thepapertiger.com.

Keys to an Effective Filing System

Whether you decide to use the software or stick with a traditional filing system, the components of an effective Reference File are still the same:

- **Mechanics**
- **Management**
- **Maintenance**

In my work with clients, I frequently discover that two of these three factors are already in operation. As soon as the third factor is incorporated, their system starts to work.

File Mechanics

The importance of the mechanics of a filing system is often overlooked. Few people enjoy filing; most can't stand it. There are three main reasons:

- **They dislike deciding** where to file the papers;
- **They dislike the physical discomfort** of jamming hands into overstuffed file drawers; or
- **They dislike the annoyance** of looking into numerous file drawers before they find the file they need.

YOUR FILE CABINET. Selecting the right file cabinet is important. My first choice, without a doubt, is a good-

SPECIAL MECHANICS

Here are some additional tips that will make the mechanics of your filing easier.

- **Avoid using paper clips in files.** They take up more space and, more importantly, catch on papers when you file them, obstructing the file label. Instead, use staples to keep together papers that are related. Also keep a staple remover handy.

- **File papers so that the most recent ones are at the front.** When you open the file you can immediately see the latest action or information. This will also make cleaning the file take less time because the oldest information will automatically be at the back.

- **Arrange the file folders alphabetically** (unless you are using The Paper Tiger numerical system). Try this idea even if you've resisted it in the past. You'll be surprised at how much more quickly you will be able to find the file you are looking for.

- **Label the outside of the file cabinet as to its contents,** either by subject, alphabet, or range of numbers. This will save you opening the third drawer when the file you want is in the second.

quality full-suspension file cabinet. "Full suspension" means that you can open the drawers all the way so no files are obstructed from view.

There are two types of file cabinets, vertical and lateral, which are distinguished by how they open. Vertical cabinets are generally 28" high, 15" wide and 26" deep. The drawer pulls out the full depth of the cabinet, and files are arranged from front to back. Lateral file cabinets are generally 28" high and 18" deep and come in widths of 30", 36", or 42". The depth is approximately 35" when the drawer is open, and the files can be arranged front to back in rows or side to side. Any good office-supply store will have a catalog in which you can see pictures of the various options, even if they do not have them in stock.

Decide whether to purchase letter- or legal-size files. Many filing systems are adjustable. I prefer letter size unless your life is complicated with many legal issues and you have a substantial amount of legal-size paper. Letter-size cabinets take up less space, and you'll save money on the cost of the file folders.

For most households a two-drawer, full-suspension

vertical cabinet will be enough. If you want to create additional working space in your work area, a two-drawer full-suspension lateral file would be a good choice. If you want or need more filing space, you can purchase a four or five-drawer file.

You can find less-expensive file cabinets at a discount store, but I don't recommend them for files you use frequently. Filing boxes are often more accessible than a poorly made metal cabinet. Keep in mind that a good quality file cabinet is a lifetime investment. Prices vary dramatically, so comparison shop after you find the cabinet you want.

If you don't have room for a traditional filing cabinet or you feel it doesn't fit with your interior décor, there are other options ranging from cardboard or plastic file boxes to solid wood cabinets designed to coordinate with your furniture. Portable file folders work if you use your kitchen or dining-room table as a workspace and want to move the files with you when you work. They also work well for files that you need access to only occasionally, and that you store in the basement, attic, garage or some other out-of-the-way place.

YOUR CHOICE OF FILE FOLDERS. You might be surprised to discover that another big decision is what kind of file folders you will use. There are several options.

Hanging files, such as those made by Pendaflex (www.Pendaflex.com) are my preference, as they are well made and the glue lasts, so you don't end up with papers in the bottom of your file cabinet. Although they are more expensive than manila folders, these folders will last significantly longer, and the plastic stand-up tabs make the labels much easier to read.

If your filing cabinet doesn't accommodate hanging files, you can purchase a hanging-file frame that can be sized to fit your file drawer.

You don't need to put manila file-folders inside the hanging files, but there are a few situations when it is advisable to do so. Sometimes you may need to take material away from home to use it. For example, you could use a manila folder to keep a file for a committee on which

If you're using manila files, buy the kind that are reinforced across the top. They will last longer and cause fewer paper cuts.

you serve so you can take the information in the folder with you to the meeting. If you do use two folders, label the hanging file and the manila file identically. This will make it easy to return the file to its proper place.

You could also use manila folders within a hanging file when you need to make subdivisions in the file. For example, the hanging folder could be labeled Car, and the manila folders could be labeled Car Insurance, Car Repairs, etc.

If you're using manila files, buy the kind that are reinforced across the top. They will last longer and cause fewer paper cuts. You can crease the fold lines at the bottom of the folder to increase its capacity and prevent obstruction of the file label.

Another type is the box-bottom file, which is useful for very thick files, or a file that has many subdivisions. These have a one-half to three-inch-wide cardboard strip in the bottom.

File folders come in a variety of colors. The hanging folders sometimes come with colored plastic tabs, but in the case of the darker colors, such as red and blue, consider substituting clear plastic tabs so that the labels are easier to read, particularly if you use typed labels.

Plastic tabs can go on the front or back of hanging files. Most people put them on the back, probably because it is consistent with the label on the back of manila folders. Try putting them on the front instead. The big advantage of having the label on the front is that when you are filing a piece of paper and you grab the plastic tab the file automatically opens to the place you need to file the paper. Use whichever method you prefer, but be consistent.

There are also many other kinds of file folders available. If you have no filing cabinet but have shelf space, use file folders with labels on the narrow end instead of on the top. Then you can put your files on shelves and still see the labels easily.

Some people like to use file folders with metal fasteners so that the papers can be punched and put in the file in chronological order and will stay that way. In most instances I find that the results are not worth the effort.

Over and over again, I have seen filing pile up because it took too much time and effort to get the holes punched.

ABLE LABELS. Labeling is the key to an effective filing system. Often I find files with penciled labels—or no label at all because they are only "temporary" files. But often, files become like the temporary building on my college campus that served as the music building for 27 years. It is very simple to use peel-off file labels so that if you need to change the label you can do so easily. In the meantime, you have a file you can easily find.

Determine what the label should say by asking: "If I wanted to find this information again what word would I think of?"

I often handwrite file labels because it's quick. I print labels in capital letters because that creates the most consistent, readable appearance. Portable label printers are widely available in prices starting at $50. These are excellent for labeling all kinds of items around your household. If you hand-label your files, use a dark-colored felt-tip pen of medium thickness. One client attaches a pen inside the file cabinet so she can always find it.

Some people like to color-code their files, and there are lots of ways to do so. You could use colored file folders, colored file labels, colored dots to stick on labels, or colored pens to write labels. Color is very useful if it tells a story. For example, you could use red labels on any files that contain information you will need at tax time, or you could use a different color label or file folder for each member of the family.

However, if it's not used consistently, color can also be confusing and very frustrating when you want to make a file quickly but can't find the right color label, pen or dot. I would caution you to use color sparingly unless you have someone to help you with the file mechanics or you particularly enjoy doing it yourself.

Whatever type of file folder you choose, put the key word at the left of the label when writing or typing labels. For example, Education—John—2002 rather than 2002—Education—John. Keep the system simple

> **I often handwrite file labels because it's quick. I print labels in capital letters because that creates the most consistent, readable appearance.**

enough so that you can maintain it as you go.

TOO MANY SYSTEMS. One of the temptations—and most frequent mistakes—in setting up a filing system is to create too many systems. In doing this you create more work for yourself. If you are looking for information, you first have to remember which filing system it is in and then determine where it is in the system. If you are trying to file information, you may find it difficult to determine which system is appropriate for that information. Unless there is a clear-cut identity, such as all files involving financial information, keep all files together in one A-Z system. Then if you are looking for Entertaining, you will go directly to "E," instead of wondering whether you put it in the personal files or the house files.

File Management

One reason people resist filing papers is a fear that they will make a poor decision and file the paper in an inappropriate or hard-to-remember file. If you are using *Taming the Paper Tiger* software, you can use an unlimited number of words or phrases to describe what you put in a file, and you don't have to worry about how you organize the files within the system. Here are some guidelines that will help you with your filing decisions:

- **Ask yourself, "Under what circumstances would I want this information?"** Be specific. "Just in case" won't help you find it again. If the answer is, "I might want this information if I were writing a speech," then save the information in a Speech Ideas file. If you answer, "I'll need this when I sell the house," then a House— Main Street file might be a good choice.

- **Ask yourself, "If I wanted this information, what word would first enter my mind?"** The answer to that question will tell you what Reference File is appropriate for this piece of paper. For example, a flyer about ordering candy from a specialty company could be filed under Gift Ideas or Mail Order Information. And invitations from a past party could be filed under Party Ideas, Printing Ideas or Mementos.

SAMPLE REFERENCE FILE INDEX

Art Owned	Hobbies	Maps/Directions
Articles	Holidays	Party records
Book Information	Home Decorating	Personal Property
Car Maintenance	Household Maintenance	Quotes
Childcare	Humor	Recreation
Church/Synagogue	Income Tax	Résumé
Consumer Information	Insurance—Car	Retirement
Credit Cards	Insurance—Household	Safe Deposit Box
Death Information	Insurance—Life	Services
Diet	Insurance—Medical	Shopping
Entertainment	Bills to be submitted	Special Interests
Education Records	Bills submitted—not paid	Subscriptions/Memberships
Financial Records	Bills paid	Stocks
Gardening/Plants	Inventory	Travel
Gift Ideas	IRA	Warranties

- **File information according to how you will use it, not where you got it.** For example, your local homeowner's association published an article recommending repair services in the area. Suppose you wake up one morning to discover that you have no hot water. What are the chances you'd remember that article in the Homeowner's Association file? A file labeled Services—Household Repair might be more useful.

- **Put all papers in their most general category first.** For example, try keeping all of your warranties and instructions in a single file. Then, if the file becomes too bulky, break it down into Warranties and Instructions—Appliances, Warranties and Instructions—Clothing, etc.

- **It's easier to look through one file with 20 pieces of paper than ten files with two papers in each;** fewer places to look, fewer places to lose. The added advantage is that when you are using a file to get a particular piece of paper you remember, you will also discover other pieces of paper you have forgotten. As a result
continued on page 72

FOR YOUR REFERENCE FILES

The following is a list of the kinds of information that can be put in a home filing system. Detailed information about what could go into the files can be found in the chapters in Part 2, Strategies for Paper Management. The categories are listed here alphabetically, as you would file them. As you read about categories you could use—and think of others that are not listed here—jot them down in the sample File Index on page 69.

Art Owned. Could also be filed under Personal Property or Insurance.

Articles. Could be divided into categories by subject, e.g. Articles—Psychology.

Book Information. This could be divided into categories such as Books—Novels, Books—History, etc.

Car Maintenance. Keep copies of all receipts from work done on your car, along with the manual that came with the car when you bought it. Information could also be filed under Automobile or Ford.

Child-Care Information. Include summer-camp information and photocopies of blank forms to be filled out with information for the sitter. Information could also be filed under Babysitter or Camp.

Church/Synagogue. This could be listed under specific name: Calvary Church,

Temple Zion, for example.

Consumer Information. If this file becomes too bulky, divide it into categories such as Consumer Information—Electronics, Consumer Information—Real Estate, etc.

Credit Cards. For each account, enter card number, address, and phone number to call if card is lost. (Keep a duplicate copy of the list in your safe deposit box.)

Death Information. What to do in case of your death or a relative's. Include a copy of wills. (Keep originals with your attorney or in a fireproof box. In some states the safe deposit box may be sealed upon your death.)

Diet Information. This could also be placed under Health or Nutrition.

Entertainment. Put ideas here for outings for family or house guests. This could be divided into categories.

Education Records. Make one file for each member of the family.

Financial Records. Separate general financial-planning information from your personal information. This file could contain information about loans, mortgages, investments, etc.

Gardening and Plants

Gift Ideas

Hobbies. Divide into specific areas such as Gardening, Coins, etc.

Holidays. File ideas for gifts, record of gifts given, ideas for next year, copies of the annual letter you send to friends and family, etc.

Home Decorating. Divide into specific areas if too bulky for one file.

Household Maintenance Records

Humor. Favorite Cartoons, Jokes, Articles

Income-Tax Information. Divide this file into subfiles for each tax year. Keep all records you may need in case of an audit. These include records of donations, taxes paid, receipts for any tax-deductible items. (See Chapter 14 for information on how long you need to keep these records.)

Insurance. You will need several files for this important category. Keep one for Car, another for Household/Personal Property (including receipts for art, jewelry, furs, etc.), a third for Life and a fourth for Medical, which in turn should be broken down into 3 folders—Bills to Be Submitted (keep blank forms here), Bills Submitted But Not Paid, and Bills Paid.

Inventory. List items in various storage areas of your home or in other locations.

IRA. This information could be included in Retirement Information, or perhaps with Financial Records.

Maps and Instructions. Directions to friends' homes, photocopies of map to your home.

Party Records. Guest lists, menus of past parties and ideas for future ones.

Personal Property. Specifics on valuables owned, if not already in Insurance file.

Quotes and Favorite Articles. This could also be called Speech Ideas if you make frequent public appearances.

Recreation. This file can be divided into various sports and activities.

Résumé

Retirement Information. Keep your latest pension statement and the annual social security statement of benefits here. If you're enrolled in other pension plans from former employers, also keep information on those accounts here. IRA and Keogh statements could be filed here as well.

Safe Deposit Box. Keep a list of what is located there. Also use this file for temporary storage of items to take to your safe deposit box.

Services. This file could be divided into

continued on page 72

FOR YOUR REFERENCE FILES (continued)

Personal and Household for information such as hair stylist, physical therapist, plumber, electrician, etc.

Shopping Information. Mail-order information, clippings about new stores, and brochures are filed here.

Special Interests. Divide this file into categories such as History, Psychology.

Subscriptions and Memberships. Keep records of renewals and order forms here.

Stocks, Bonds and Mutual Funds. Divide into separate subfiles for each investment you own. Keep broker statements here, along with annual reports. Also make a separate file here for information on stocks, bonds or mutual funds you're considering buying.

Travel. If you have a lot of information here, divide the file into geographic areas.

Warranties and Instructions. If this file becomes too bulky, use a box-bottom file (see page 66) or divide it into types, e.g., Major Appliances, Lawn Tools, or Home Electronics.

you will be able to use more of the information you file.

■ **If a paper could be filed in more than one place, choose the one you are most likely to look in first.** Write a note on the other file folders that says, "See also . . ." If you feel it is essential, make a copy for the second file.

■ **Organize your files consistently.** For example, you may have medical and educational records for several members of the family. Decide whether you want all of John's files together; i.e., John—Education, John—Medical, or all medical files together, i.e., Medical—Ann, Medical—John.

■ **Group like files together.** Whenever you have files you want to keep together physically in your file system, find a word that encompasses all the files. For example, instead of having a file that says Biking under "B" and Skiing under "S", you could have Recreation—Biking and Recreation—Skiing.

FILE INDEX. A File Index is the final and perhaps the most important step in managing your files. The same information can be filed several ways. For example, I could file information about my car in Automobile, Car, Chrysler, or Vehicle. The problem comes if you file information under Car one time and under Chrysler the next—and your spouse looks for it under Automobile.

This dilemma can be avoided by making an alphabetical list of all file names, with cross references to files that contain related material. *Taming the Paper Tiger* software will automatically generate a File Index, as well as other useful reports. When you are writing or typing the index, leave space between each letter of the alphabet so you will have room to add new file titles as you need them. Put as many names on one page as possible; use columns if necessary. It's unlikely you'll ever get to the filing if you have to read a 15-page guide first. (See the sample File Index on page 69. The categories shown are described on pages 70-72. Use this sample as your starting point by crossing out categories you won't need and adding in those you will.)

Keep your File Index accessible in hard copy in the front of your filing system or at your desk. Make changes with pen or pencil. Or keep the list in your computer so you can update it quickly and easily. When you read an article you want to file, check the index to see what file already exists that might be appropriate for that particular article.

Use the index if you are looking for an article. It is much easier to check a File Index to see where you might find an article than it is to open the file drawer and go through file after file.

The index is particularly important if you are learning a new system or if more than one person will be using the same system. Keep in mind also that if there is a particular piece of paper you are afraid of losing, you can list it on the index. For example, Birth Certificate—See Legal Information.

SAMPLE HEADINGS FOR YOUR SYSTEM. You may wish to organize your files into various categories. A friend of mine divides her files into three categories: Financial and legal, Reference, and Children. Some people put all files that involve payments of any kind into one category and all other files in a reference category.

Be aware that there are always gray areas when you begin categorizing. For example, you might think of Medical as a distinct Reference File or something to be filed in a Financial folder. You can eliminate the problem of determining what category a file should be in by filing everything strictly by the alphabet. Then if you are looking for Medical, there is no question of where to look.

Keep in mind also that your filing system will change as your life circumstances change. For example, if you get married you will need to decide whether to maintain two separate filing systems or combine them into one. If you decide to combine them, you may want to use color to identify files that belong specifically to one person. (But color coding can also cause problems, as discussed earlier in this chapter.)

File Maintenance

No matter how much time and energy you spend creating a system to fit your particular needs, you will still need to adopt a plan to maintain the system. The following steps will help.

DETERMINE WHEN—OR IF—YOU WILL DO THE FILING. More and more professional people are recognizing that it is cost effective to hire someone else to do the routine household management tasks—including filing—just as we hire others to maintain the lawn.

If you will be doing your own filing, decide how you will keep the to-file pile from becoming larger than the file cabinet. Some people file when they pay bills. That way, two potentially unpleasant tasks are done at the same time, and they can reward themselves with a more pleasant activity when they're finished. Other people wait until the to-file box is full.

People procrastinate about filing because they don't like deciding where the paper should be filed. That decision is easier to make when you have just read the letter or article. If you circle the key word or write it in the upper right-hand corner before you put the paper in the to-file box or your Action File, the filing task will be only a mechanical one and will take less time.

This method is essential if someone else does your filing because no two people would necessarily put a paper in the same file. A paper relating to car insurance, for example, could be filed under Car or Insurance. In this instance, the File Index is invaluable.

CLEAN OUT FILES AS YOU USE THEM. I cannot count how many times I've seen clients with a paper in hand they knew could be tossed say, "I'll have to clean this out someday," and promptly put the piece of paper back into the file again instead of directly into the wastebasket.

ESTABLISH AN ANNUAL FILE CLEAN-OUT DAY. Around tax time is frequently a good time, since you will be looking into many of your files then anyway. An alternative is to wait until you need the file space. As long as you have room to file papers easily the issue of purging is not a major one. But when you neglect filing the paper you would like to file because it is physically uncomfortable or downright impossible to get your fingers into the file cabinet, then the time for Clean-Out Day has arrived! (If you use the *Taming the Paper Tiger* software, be sure to generate a File Retention Worksheet to make your file clean-out easier.)

How Long Is Enough?

Determine how long you need to keep the papers you file. Date information when you file it so it will be easy to tell if it is recent enough to be useful. In certain cases, such as a file of newsletters, you can put the retention information right on the file label (for example, Community Newsletter—Keep one year).

The issue of retention guidelines is a difficult one. In many instances the decision is purely discretionary. How long do you want to keep articles you intend to read, or reviews of restaurants? In other cases, you should simply keep material forever, updating the information as necessary. This would include birth certificates, wills, insurance policies, school and medical records, etc.

There are legal reasons for keeping other material for a certain amount of time. This material mostly deals with financial and tax matters. For quick reference to see how long you should keep what, turn to the chart in the Appendix.

There are other factors to consider in making your decision about retaining material. One is space. If you have enough of it (say, a basement) to keep everything—and it doesn't make you feel uncomfortable to have that paper laying around—then ignore it. Be sure the material is well organized—and make sure to separate the archival materials from those you are currently using.

But even if you have ample room for storage, if you get a knot in your stomach every time you open the file drawer or closet door, the price you are paying for your failure to make decisions about paper retention is high, and you should look for alternatives.

Your Action Files

Clients with great piles of paper on their desks will frequently say, "I need all of this on my desk because I am working on it." But often a close look will determine that even though all the papers on the desk might need to be saved (although that's not always true, either), not all of them are necessary to complete the projects being worked on. A bulky Action File often indicates that some of those papers could go in a Reference File, or you may need two or more Action Files for one project, such as Party—Menus and Party—Invitations.

If you lead a very simple lifestyle you may find that one file called Action is all you need, but for many people a pile of papers that need action would soon topple over. When the pile gets that deep, it is difficult to do anything. It soon takes as much time to find a project as it does to do it.

The Next Step

Remember that clutter is postponed decisions. To simplify the decision-making process, it is helpful to recognize that the papers we need to take action on fall into two basic categories. I call them temporary actions and permanent actions. Temporary actions are things you are going to do that will come to an end. These might include a trip you will be taking, a party you are planning, or a purchase you're going to make. Permanent actions are those you do over and over again, such as making phone calls, paying bills or writing letters.

To determine the permanent-action categories into which a particular piece of paper falls, ask yourself, "What is the next action I need to take on this piece of paper?" It is crucial that you recognize the significance of the word "next" in this question. The answer will tell you into which action file to put the paper. There are several possible answers to the question, and each answer is an Action-File category.

Sometimes it takes time to find the answer. For example, you have received a letter from Joe with a question about changing the membership qualifications for an association to which you belong. Your initial reaction may be, "I have to call Joe," but you realize you need to speak with Nancy first to get her opinion, but you can't talk intelligently to her until you've read the association's bylaws.

Joe's letter requires three actions: read the bylaws; call Nancy; and call Joe. You would therefore first put the letter in your Call Action File, with a temporary note on it to Call Nancy and Call Joe. Then make an appointment with yourself (noted in your calendar) to Read bylaws. Add "C-Nancy/C-Joe" to the note as a reminder that you're reading the bylaws to get information you can discuss in a call to Nancy before you call Joe.

The box on pages 80-83 describes several possible Action-File categories. The major advantage to this system of file categories is an increased ability to manage your time effectively. It is a good time-management practice to group like activities together. Then, when you have ten minutes before a business meeting at work or before you need to meet your child at school, a quick look in Call can help you use those ten minutes to your advantage. Or if you're going to an appointment where you may have to wait, take along Write with some stationery for personal notes or some scratch paper to draft more formal correspondence.

Logistics Strategy

You may be feeling swamped at this point! Anything new can seem overwhelming, so don't despair too early in the game. Try one or two Action Files to begin—Calls Expected is a favorite of many of my clients.

One question you may have is "Where do I put all these files?" If you're an out of sight, out of mind person, you'll want to keep them visible. There are a variety of file-folder containers for manila or hanging files that you can put on the top of your desk. If you prefer the clean-desk look, put them in a filing drawer in your desk, if there is one, or in a portable file box under or near your desk.

As you experiment with the system, you'll discover that each category does not have to be a file per se; nor does it have to be on your desk. For example, I know of no one whose Read category will fit into a file folder, and most people don't read at their work area. So Read could be in a basket beside your easy chair or the bed, or even in the bathroom—or, most likely, a combination (see Chapter 15 for more detailed information on Read). You may want to keep Photocopy in a folder near the door or in your briefcase so you will have it when you go out.

If the thought of creating a system like this yourself is overwhelming, check out www.ProductiveEnvironment.com to purchase a Paper Tiger Action File Kit.

All Those Files!

Now, you might be asking "How do I remember to look in all those files?" Try it. You can put a symbol on your calendar to remind you. In many instances, such as Call, there will undoubtedly be one call you'll automatically remember to make. When you check the file for information on that call, you will be reminded of the others you want to make.

You may be confused with the similarity of the categories for the to-do list (Chapter 8) and the Action Files. Sometimes your to do is just a thought, in which case you write it in your calendar or on your to-do (or on a piece of paper in your Action File). Other times, the to-do involves a piece of paper that goes in the Action File. It is not a duplication, unless you choose to use a duplication system as an insurance policy.

FOR YOUR ACTION FILES

Here are descriptions of a number of categories for action. Don't be intimidated by the number of categories; you probably won't need them all—and you might decide you need others that aren't included here. Note in the space provided categories you think you can use.

If, as you read the list, the whole idea begins to seem overwhelming, choose a few categories that have particular appeal to you and try them. If you're anything like the thousands of people who have adopted the system, you'll soon love it and wonder how you ever managed without it.

Calls. The next action required on a piece of paper is often a telephone call to someone. In addition to putting the paper in the Call file, you may wish to make a note on your calendar on the day you need to make the call. Using a symbol such as "C" will remind you that there is additional information in the Call file.

Calls Expected. How many times have you received a telephone call in which the conversation began, "Hello. This is Anne Smith. I am returning your call." A knot forms in your stomach as you frantically try to remember why you called her—or even who she is! But if you have a note in your Calls Expected file that tells you why you have left a message for that person to return your call, it can be a real stress-saver.

In addition, you can review the file periodically to check the current status of the calls. Were you simply returning her call, and the ball is now in her court, or do you really want to talk to her? If the former, after a period of time throw the paper out. If the latter, take the paper out of Calls Expected and put it in Call, with a note on your calendar to make the call again.

Computer Entry. Some of the papers on your desk contain information that needs to be entered into your computer. It will be more efficient to make several entries at the same time—or delegate it to someone else to enter. When you've entered the material from this file into the computer, either throw out the papers, pass them on to someone else who may need them, or, if you must save them, move them to the appropriate Reference File.

Why, you may ask, if I'm helping you tame your paper tiger, would I suggest you keep paper after you've entered the information in your computer? The simple answer is that there are instances when you need to keep the paper. For example, you might track your investments on a computer, but you still need records of transactions for tax purposes. Be very careful what you do keep; it's all too easy to enter information and keep the paper anyway, just in case. Ask yourself, "What's the worst thing that could happen if I don't have this paper?" Can you live with the consequence? If so, toss; if not, file (for more information on using computers in your home, see Chapter 22).

Discuss. Communication is a key to managing the paper in our lives. Frequently we can't act on a matter until we have discussed it with another person. All of us have certain people in our lives with whom we routinely discuss issues, whether it is a spouse, a child, a colleague or a friend, or a professional resource. The Discuss category can contain several subcategories. For example, Discuss—Mary, Discuss—Accountant. If you need to discuss a particular piece of paper by a specific time, put a reminder in your calendar.

File. People dislike filing and will put it off as long as possible. Even if you don't mind filing, but the file cabinet is in another room, you will need a File category for those pieces of paper that need to go into the Reference Files. Many of the pieces of paper that arrive in the mail can go directly into File and never clutter the top of your desk (for more information, see Chapter 10).

Pay. This is the category to put all the bills you need to pay, as well as any other paper that requires writing a check, an order you wish to place or a donation you would like to make. If your household finances are quite complicated, you may want to subdivide this category. For example, you could have a Must Pay for

mortgage, utilities and car payment and a Would Like to Pay for potential donations, orders, subscriptions. If you pay some of the bills and your spouse pays others, you might consider subdividing the category into Pay—Betty and Pay—Bob. This is also a good place to put payment-coupon books and reminders of deductions that are automatically taken from your checking account.

Pending. Many of my clients have found this category particularly helpful. Many names have been applied to this category—Suspension, Tickler or Bring Up are some examples. Clients often describe a piece of paper to me by saying, "This is pending. I haven't decided yet." Wrong! That's procrastination. Pending papers are papers that will require action at some future date, or that will require action after you have received additional information.

When you're tempted to put a piece of paper in this category because you're uncertain of your decision, ask yourself, "What am I going to know tomorrow that I don't know today?" If the answer is "Nothing," you will know that you need to look further into the issue to find out what other category the paper really belongs in.

If you simply cannot make a decision at this time and you want to postpone the decision, put the paper in Pending, but make a note on your calendar as a reminder to consider the issue again. If

continued on page 82

FOR YOUR ACTION FILES (continued)

you receive a dinner invitation and with the invitation are directions for getting to the host's home, put the invitation in Pending with a symbol such as "P" beside the engagement notation on your calendar. (If you have many Pending items, you may want to create a 1-31 file—one for each day of the month—and put the piece of paper in the file for the day you'll need it. If you check your Pending file each day, it isn't necessary to put the cross-referenced note in your calendar.)

Photocopy. Often you can't take the next action on a piece of paper until you make a photocopy, as in the case of submitting medical insurance claims. Another example is when you want to send a clipping from the local newspaper to your sister, but you also want a copy for yourself.

Projects. If you have several small projects going at once, you could keep the information for all of them in one file, or you might prefer to keep a separate file for each one. Those projects that are currently active fall into the Action-File category while those that are completed or have been put on hold temporarily go into the Reference-File category.

If the project involves many papers, it may be appropriate to have a Reference File and an Action File. The Action File would contain only those papers you need to complete the current step of the project. When that step is completed, review the materials in the file, discard what you don't need and return the rest to the Reference File. Then move the papers relating to the next step of the project to the Action File. Project files should be arranged alphabetically.

Special Events. If you enjoy many outings—concerts, lectures, sports events—but have difficulty keeping track of them, consider keeping a separate Events Calendar. When you receive a notice of an upcoming event, list it there. Be sure, of course, to put definite commitments on your master calendar. Other options are to have a folder labeled Schedules in which you put these notices, or to hang them on the bulletin board. Then if you have a free evening you can check the folder to see what options you have. This is particularly helpful if you have out-of-town guests and you are assisting them in planning their schedules or you want to entertain them.

Take to Office/Home. Designate a particular place to put those papers (and other items) you need to take with you to work. Choose a convenient location—on a table near the door, for example. Try keeping your briefcase at the same spot so that you can put things right in. If your briefcase is not in the usual spot, put the item where your briefcase should be. Then when you return the briefcase it will be easy to get them together. This will stop the frustrating game of having one and not the other, and vice versa. Have a similar setup in your office.

Upcoming Meetings/Trips. Virtually every time you plan to go to a meeting or take a trip you will accumulate papers related to that event, whether it is an airplane ticket, a meeting agenda or a note from a friend asking you to call or visit when you are in the city.

When the trip or meeting is over, throw away those pieces of paper that are no longer essential and file the remaining papers according to how you will use them next. For example, the letter from your friend might contain an address that could be entered in your phone listing and then the letter could be tossed. Or you may wish to put the letter in your Mementos box to read again in the years to come (see Chapter 18).

Write/E-mail. Sometimes writing a letter or sending an e-mail is the next action to take. This category includes business communications, personal notes, thank-yous and special-occasion cards.

If writing is a problem area for you, think about what you can do to make the task easier. Many people find it helps to physically separate these categories. Sometimes you may feel like spending ten minutes writing a thank-you note but not an hour writing an old college roommate. If you have to dig through a huge pile to find what interests you at the moment, you may lose interest before you find it.

I use airport waiting time to shop for greeting cards I like. Because I keep a supply of favorites on hand, sending a congratulations card literally takes only minutes—and I'm sure doing it makes me feel every bit as good as the person to whom I send it.

Keep postcards on hand for quick notes. Many people now write responses on the bottom of business letters and return them to the sender to speed response time—and save paper. If you need a copy, put the paper in Photocopy or Take to Office.

If you are procrastinating about writing a letter, ask yourself if a phone call would suffice, or at least get the process started. Or write an outline for yourself to help organize your thoughts and make the letter less difficult to write.

Strategies for
Paper Management

Papers for Proof, Pleasure and Pondering

Y ou can manage every piece of paper in your life by using the techniques described in the previous chapters. However, there are several categories of papers that particularly plague many households.

There are essential papers relating to paying taxes and bills and for keeping family records. And there are other kinds of paper that seem to multiply like mushrooms all over the house—maps, coupons, flyers from local businesses, and instruction books that come with new electronic gadgets, kitchen appliances and garden tools.

Activities create more paper—travel, family celebrations, seminars, recreation and sports events. Medical emergencies, educational pursuits, career changes, job responsibilities, religious affiliations, club memberships, and community involvement add still more paper.

Contributing to the accumulation are photographs and other family mementos, recipes, books, and articles from magazines and newspapers to which you want to refer in the future.

And let's not forget about the papers relating to your children—papers that you need to keep about them, papers they need to keep relating to the management of their own lives, and still more papers you or they want to save as memories of their achievements.

You will undoubtedly have questions about certain pieces of paper and will discover a variety of ways you could handle them. How do you know which is best?

No Right or Wrong Way

Remember, there is no right or wrong way to organize anything. If you asked three interior designers to re-design your living room, you would obviously get three different results. You might like all three plans, but proba-bly one of them would appeal to you more than the oth-ers. If you asked three different people to write a newspaper article about a community event, you would undoubtedly get three different stories. They would prob-ably all be accurate but each would be colored by the per-sonal experiences and views of the individual authors.

Paper management has this same variety and flexi-bility. The next chapters will discuss some of the major areas of paper management that you face in your life. You will find different approaches for handling these challenges, along with some of the pros and cons for each method. Choose the way that sounds the most fea-sible to you. Be sure to give it a fair try.

Many people fail in setting up new systems because they do not allow enough time to develop the new habits that are necessary to make any kind of change in their life. Try the new system for a reasonable amount of time—two to three months is usually adequate. If the system is still not working, ask yourself these questions: "Is the problem that I don't have enough time? If so, what can I do to make the time?" "Am I having problems with the me-chanics? If so, who can help me?" "Do I really want to do this? If not, is there anyone else who can do it? Or, what would happen if I didn't do it? What would I do then?"

Often, all that is required for success is a modifica-tion of the system. Spend some time identifying what you liked about the system you tried and what you did not. With that information, you can move on to make the nec-essary changes to create a system that will work for you.

Who's in Charge Here?

One of the questions that inevitably arises in every household is who is going to manage the paper? There's likely to be a major conflict if no one in the family is willing to do it, or if there's a disagreement about how the paper should be handled.

Communication and negotiation are the keys to success in family paper-management. In most households, specific responsibilities are assigned to specific people. One person may pay bills, while another does the filing. Or, a husband and wife may elect to pick a "bill-paying night" and do it together.

If one person generally does the filing, other family members should know about the system in case that person is ill or away. If someone tears out a newspaper article for filing, that same person should identify where to file it if he or she expects to be able to find it again (see Chapter 10). In fact, every member of the household will have papers to handle. Children need to learn to take care of their own papers to help them learn to be independent.

If one family member is more skilled in paper management—or more willing to learn—the entire family will benefit. In that case, the paper manager should be excused from doing some other household chores such as shopping errands or household or outdoor maintenance.

As with any attempt at learning something new, you'll discover stumbling blocks. Don't let that stop you. In every organizing process, things will seem worse before they get better. A natural outcome of sorting through piles of papers is a renewed awareness that we are not as productive as we would like to be. Concentrate on how you are going to improve the situation now, not on what you should have done in the past.

How Does It Make You Feel?

Sometimes my clients have a great deal of difficulty letting go of the excess in their lives, whether it is paper, clothes, kitchen utensils or their children's outgrown toys. If that's true in your case, ask the question, "How does having this make me feel?" If the answer is anything negative—sad, angry, guilty—then decide whether you want to continue to surround yourself with anything that makes you feel that way.

Often our willingness to let go of something increas-

Communication and negotiation are the keys to success in family paper-management.

DISASTER-PROOF YOUR IMPORTANT PAPERS

In case you have to evacuate your home in an emergency, keep copies of your most vital papers in a portable container you can easily take with you. These would include:

- Birth certificates and adoption records
- Marriage certificates and divorce decrees
- Drivers' licenses
- Passports/Visas/Green cards
- Social Security cards
- Titles, deeds and registrations for property owned
- Wills and trust documents
- Mortgage and loan information
- Insurance policies
- Bank account records
- Investment account records
- Credit card numbers

Keep original copies of difficult-to-replace documents, such as birth certificates and titles, in a safe deposit box. Make sure the box is held in more than one person's name. While information regarding bank accounts, insurance policies, and investments can be reproduced from account numbers, having immediate access to hard copy may be helpful.

Keep a list of all the documents you have and where they are located. Make sure that those who need access to them know where to find this master list. Kiplinger's *Your Family Records Organizer* (www.kiplinger.com/organizer; 800-280-7165, Operator 89) is a CD-ROM product created to help you keep track of all these documents.

Key contact numbers to carry in your wallet: Doctor. . . employer/spouse's employer. . . children's schools. . . banks. . . insurance agents. . . minister, rabbi or priest. . . close relatives, friends and neighbors. . . utility companies . . . alarm-system company.

es if we can identify other people who need it more than we do (for more information, see Chapter 23). Local newspapers sometimes list organizations that need donations of clothes, appliances and other items. Keep a list of these in your Reference File or rotary file.

The clarity of our goals and our willingness to look at the future instead of dwelling on the past is another important factor in our ability to make decisions about what we need to keep. If you find yourself unable to make progress with letting go of things you know deep down inside you really don't need, it might be a symptom of a deeper problem. You may even wish to seek professional help in setting some specific goals in your life.

Bills, Bills, Bills

We can laugh about many of the papers in our lives, but there is little humor in unpaid bills. A lost bill can mean a disconnected telephone or unnecessary service charges. Bills can represent emotionally charged issues such as the extravagant new suit that you've never worn or the vacation that fizzled.

We must not only deal with the issue of finding the money to pay bills, but we must also determine who pays them—when, where, and how. Frequently clients spend more time debating whether to postpone paying a bill than it would have taken for them to write the check. And how embarrassing it is when the mortgage company calls about your delinquent payment and you can't even find the payment book!

Keeping Track

You can reduce the stress of paying bills by establishing a method to keep track of them. The simplest method is to put all the bills in one place, pay them at least once a month, and then file all the receipts in one place, or in different places depending on the type of expense involved. If you need to refer to the payment, you will be able to find the information.

Using this method, it is not necessary to open a bill at the time you receive it. In fact, unless you plan to do something specific with the information in the bill at that time, I don't particularly recommend it. The result of just opening many bills without acting on them is a significant

If you don't pay all the bills at once, you need a method to keep track of when to pay them. Try opening them and marking the amount due and due date on the envelope.

increase in the number of pieces of paper you have to handle. More importantly, you increase the likelihood that the bill and its return envelope will get separated.

If you're not going to pay all the bills at one time, you need a good method to keep track of when to pay them. Try opening them and marking the amount due and the due date on the front of the envelope. Then put a note on your calendar on the day you need to pay the bill. Still another method is to make a list of the bills as they come in. Then you can check them off as you pay them, noting the date paid and the check number. This list can be useful for future reference.

Keeping track of your expenses and living within a budget is one of the keys to a more peaceful life. This book is not intended to be a financial-planning guide; there are several good resources on that subject at your bookstore or library, or check out www.kiplinger.com/books. The issue of tracking expenses as it relates to paper management, however, has to do with when (and where) you will record your expenses. Decide whether you will enter the information in your tracking system when you pay bills or if that is an unrealistic expectation for one sitting. If it is, determine when you will enter your expenses, just as you determined when you would pay your bills. Make an appointment with yourself and mark it in your calendar until you're in the habit of recording the information.

Time to Pay Up

A key element in creating a bill-paying system that works is recognizing that it must be done—by someone. If you hate doing it, do not assume you have to be that someone. Your spouse might not mind handling the job. More and more people are simplifying their lives by using direct-payment services offered by many financial institutions. And many others are hiring people, such as a bookkeeper or professional organizer, to pay bills and handle other routine chores so that they have time and energy for other activities that are more fun—and maybe profitable, thus providing funds to pay for the service.

A SIMPLE SOLUTION

One of the most exciting tools on the market for helping you to manage your finances is called "The Money Organizer System." This system uses a unique tool called The Money Organizer that allows you to plan your purchases in advance and carry that plan with you right in your checkbook.

You simply record the amount you have allocated for each spending category of your monthly budget right in the Money Organizer. When you make a purchase, whether by check, debit card, credit card or cash, you subtract it from the appropriate category at the point of purchase. At any given time, you have a clear picture of your spending for that month. One of the most valuable aspects of the Money Organizer is that it allows you to take an annual bill, such as a life insurance policy, and prorate it over the year. That means that when the bill arrives, the money to pay for it is already set aside in the insurance category of your Money Organizer. (For information about this product, call 800-450-4580 or check the Web site: www.moneyorganizer.com.)

If, however, you don't have the luxury of someone to help you pay your bills, what can you do to make the task more palatable? For many, the answer lies with their computer. One of the greatest inroads the computer industry has made into our homes is the area of managing finances. People who have had little interest in the computer are often motivated when they discover the power of using it to pay bills and keep track of their financial situation.

All that aside, the first step is to determine the best time to pay bills. Do you prefer to pay them once or twice a month or to pay each one as it arrives?

In the interest of financial planning, it is wiser to pay bills once a month. This method gives you the opportunity to look at your overall financial picture and to make financial decisions based on hard facts, rather than on feelings and fears. For example, if you know you can't pay off the balance on all of your credit card bills, pay the one with the highest interest rate.

However, if you know yourself well enough to recognize that you will procrastinate on a task that feels overwhelming—that is, facing a mountain of bills all at once—you may be better off paying each as it comes in.

REDUCE YOUR PAPER

One way to reduce the paper in your life is to keep fewer credit cards. You'll also save on annual fees. And try to pay off credit card bills monthly so you don't pay non-deductible interest. If you must carry a balance, make sure your card has a low interest rate. And if you own a home, think about consolidating the debt with a home equity loan, the interest on which is most likely tax deductible.

Debit cards are very popular now, eliminating the need to carry a checkbook and create paper checks. They simply work like a credit card but debit the amount directly from your account. Just be sure to keep the receipt and update your check register whenever you use the card.

A Place to Pay Up

If you pay your bills at home, choose where you will do it. If you are going to pay bills as they arrive, the location where you'll pay them must be convenient; otherwise it will be too much trouble to go there and you will not do it.

Similarly, if you pay bills once or twice a month, it is essential that you have a convenient place to put your Pay Action File so you can put bills in the folder as they come in and you're sorting the mail. This place doesn't have to be the same place where you will eventually pay the bills.

Be sure to have everything you need in your bill-paying location—stamps, a pen that works, your checkbook, return address labels, envelopes, and a place to put the receipts from the paid bills. Have a large wastebasket, recycling bin, or paper shredder within reach for all those flyers that come along with the bills with the "too good to be true" temptations!

Finally, be sure to get the stamped bills to a place where you will see them so they actually get to the mailbox. Frequently amid my clients' piles of papers, I find checks they wrote but never mailed. Failure to mail a payment can cause frustration and confusion when you receive a delinquency notice for a bill you thought you'd paid. Your check register indicates you paid it. You remember writing the check. Did it get lost in the mail? Did the company make a mistake? Only when your bank statement arrives, or you call the company, can you know for sure whether or not you paid the bill. And if it turns out you haven't made the payment, you also have to pay past due penalties.

Billing Statements: To Save or Not to Save

After you have paid the bills, you've got to do something with the statements. Ask yourself: "Why would I need this statement?" If you recall your past habits, you may realize that you have indeed never used the information. You might then decide to throw the statements away, knowing that you can always refer to your canceled checks and check register.

You could keep a record of payments to a particular company in case there are billing questions. Put the statements in a Reference File marked MasterCard, or Sears, or a more generic file, Bills Paid.

Another function of such a file would be to provide a record of personal expenses. For example, if you are divorced you may keep records of expenditures on children in case a problem develops with child support. If so, create a Reference File called Child Support, Children, or Financial Information—Children.

You may keep certain statements for specific, but temporary, circumstances. For example, if you plan to sell your home within the next year, keep the utility bills because the information will interest a potential buyer.

Frequently the primary reason for keeping the information is for the IRS. See the next chapter for detailed information.

Receipts: Trash or Treasure

Then there's those pesky credit card receipts and ATM receipts—flimsy little pieces of paper that you often find stuffed in your suit pockets, lying on top of your dresser and buried in your briefcase or desk drawers. What should you do with them?

IF YOU PAY BILLS AT THE OFFICE

Establish a system for getting the bills from your mailbox at home to the office. Put them in a basket near the door, in an Action File on your desk or directly into your briefcase. You can also arrange to have the bills mailed directly to your office.

Keep in mind that the main purpose of those credit card receipts is to make sure you have been billed properly and to use as proof of purchase in the event you need to make a return or exchange. One simple method is to get several business-size envelopes—one for each credit card. Put the name of one card on each envelope and, if you have the space, hang the envelopes on a bulletin board with the flap tucked inside to create a pocket. When you return home, put receipts in the appropriate envelopes. When the credit card bills arrive, you can match them up with the receipts in minutes and pay the bills. (The envelope method also works well for bank statements.)

Some receipts must be retained for tax and other financial record-keeping purposes. Other reasons you should keep a receipt include major purchases that have a warranty, tax-deductible items, or a property-improvement expense.

The Tax Man Cometh

Someone once said that to live comfortably it's not how much you earn, but how much you keep after taxes. You might hate to pay them, think the system is unfair, dislike the forms, and stage a mini-tax rebellion, but in the end the tax man cometh—sometimes with penalty!

It's April 7. You haven't seen the top of the dining room in two weeks because shopping bags and shoe boxes of paid bills and receipts, piles of canceled checks and unidentified cash register receipts cover it. There are more receipts in the bottom of your briefcase, the back of the dresser drawer and on your kitchen counter.

To add to the chaos, you've got a 15-page guide from your accountant with instructions on what information he or she needs. (You may visit www.kiplinger.com/managing/taxes for more information on latest tax changes.) Your head pounds and your stomach churns as the countdown begins to April 15. What can you do to minimize the stress around this deadline?

Two Kinds of Taxpayers

First, it's important to recognize that there are basically two kinds of taxpayers—those who feel comfortable only if they record deductions as they occur during the year and those who prefer to ignore the entire issue until the fear of the penalty for late payment is greater than their willingness to procrastinate.

Somewhere in our education about managing our financial affairs we heard the message that the right way to

THE LAST-MINUTE ORGANIZER

One man I know files all his receipts in two huge garbage bags—one labeled Tax Deductible and the other Non-Tax Deductible. He then ignores the issue of taxes until the deadline hovers over him and he's forced to dig in.

keep tax records is on a daily, or at least some frequent, basis. We envision a professional-looking ledger with neat entries and accurate totals at the end of each month. Most of all we dream of walking into the tax accountant's office the first week of February with everything in order!

There are many ways to maintain tax information. Some people are satisfied keeping everything together in a shoebox until the last minute. Most people require a slightly more sophisticated system. Some require a much more sophisticated system. But everyone should have some system because the more records you have, the more claims you can prove—and the more money you will save. If your records are incomplete, you're likely to pay Uncle Sam more than you legally owe.

If you have never filed your taxes before April 15, you're probably not the type of person who will conscientiously maintain daily records. Perhaps you should accept that as a reality—and plan accordingly!

Determine your style of recordkeeping and weigh the alternatives for yourself. What are the risks of postponing the task? What is the worst possible thing that could happen? What would you do in that situation? Do you need an on-going system to feel secure? Is it reasonable to design a system that requires daily entries, or is it more realistic to accept the fact that you will not deal with taxes until April?

The Ongoing System

In my experience, it's possible, and preferable, to avoid all the last-minute work if you can. What are the advantages of an on-going recordkeeping system?

A key advantage is that you are less likely to omit

legitimate expenses if you record them as they occur. You will also be able to make better financial decisions, particularly if your income varies from month to month, as in the case of many self-employed people.

An ongoing recordkeeping system also helps in case you're audited. Your chances of defending your deductions are greater if there is evidence that your expenses were noted "contemporaneously," as the IRS states it. Taxpayers are no longer permitted to re-create records months later to satisfy an audit, unless the records were destroyed in an extreme circumstance such as fire or flood.

THE ELECTRONIC METHOD

If you use your computer for managing your finances, you'll certainly want to consider a software program for preparing returns.

If you're audited, records are essential. Legitimate expenses may be disallowed for lack of documentation. If that is not enough to spur you into action, consider the high cost of interest and penalties on past-due tax.

Finally, if you've kept accurate records through the year, you'll find it easier to get your information to your tax accountant or file your forms yourself before the April rush. One of my clients routinely used to request an extension on April 15 instead of filing his return. After we worked out a recordkeeping system, not only did he file his return early for the first time in his life, he received a refund on March 15. Instead of paying a penalty for non-payment of taxes, he received an interest payment on his savings account.

If you choose to keep your records as you go, make an appointment with yourself to get it done, whether at the end of each working day, or when you pay the bills. If you record expenses on a calendar, choose one with enough space to write—or use a separate notebook. Don't let perfectionism defeat you. If you forget to record a luncheon expense at the time, decide what you can do next time. A less than perfect recordkeeping system is better than no system at all.

Keep accurate records of income from all sources— for example, your job, freelance work, and interest paid and capital gains realized from savings accounts and investments. Note the source of the income in your check register. IRS auditors frequently match deposit records to amounts declared on tax returns. If you cannot prove that a $2,000 deposit is repayment of a loan to a friend by showing a copy of your original check or other transmittal, the IRS could treat the entire amount as taxable income.

File records of deductible items such as medical bills, charitable donations or casualty losses as soon as you get them. The system that demands the least amount of work has two clearly labeled envelopes for each deductible category: expenses paid by check or credit card; cash receipts. The information in these envelopes will not be needed unless you are audited by the IRS and need additional supporting evidence.

The April Approach

It is also possible (with certain preliminary precautions) to wait until April 15 is just around the corner and still do the job effectively. It makes little difference whether you spend ten minutes a day, one hour a week, or three days a year working on taxes. If waiting until the last minute is your normal approach, accept it and plan for it. Here's a game plan that should help you out.

Even if you prefer the April Approach for organizing your records, remember that you still have to have the records available when the time comes. First collect the records—canceled checks, credit card receipts and statements, bank statements, cash register receipts, calendars, and any articles or other information you may have collected about what you can deduct—and sort them.

When all the papers have been separated into the appropriate piles, place each category into a separate container, such as a large envelope, plastic basket, or shoe box. Label each category clearly. Since you will probably need more than one sitting to complete your taxes, these labeled containers make it easier to clear your work area, if necessary, and to find your place when you are ready to continue.

Now take one category at a time. Eliminate duplicate receipts; for example, keep either the customer

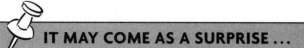

IT MAY COME AS A SURPRISE ...

Most taxpayers don't really have to file by April 15 because they don't owe a dime on their returns. There's no penalty for missing the deadline if you are due a refund. But don't wait too long! You've already given the IRS an interest-free loan on the money due to you. You still have to file a return; failing to do so until after the IRS figures you are late—and asks you about it— could mean a penalty.

copy of a credit card payment or the copy sent with your monthly statement, or staple the receipts together. Always keep the receipt with the most complete information. If you need to correlate your charges with your calendar to prove a tax-deductible expense, such as in the case of entertainment, put all receipts in chronological order to speed up the process.

Preparing to File

Whether you keep your papers organized through the year or you wait to organize them when you do your taxes, the rest of the process is the same. Use a calculator with a tape to total the receipts for each category of deductible items and staple the tape to each pile. Write the category on the tape. If you use an accountant, make an itemized list of your deductions so the accountant can double-check your work, and so it will be easier to support your claim in the case of an audit.

While you've held most of the information concerning your deductions through the year, other records of deductions and documents regarding your income will be supplied by others, so watch your mail carefully. Mixed in with the usual junk are documents critical for your tax return. These include:

- **a W-2 form** from your employer, if you work for wages;
- **a 1098** detailing how much mortgage interest you paid;
- **1099 forms,** if you are an independent contractor, own stock that paid dividends, or had interest or other

types of non-wage income. If you have kept good records, you can match the 1099s against them. This double-check not only helps catch any errors; it also keeps you from overlooking taxable income if the 1099 doesn't show up. If the IRS gets a copy of a 1099 and you don't, their computers will spot the under-payment and audit you for the money, plus interest and possible penalties.

Now you are ready to begin entering the information on the tax forms, or to take the information to your accountant. (Many accountants will provide a worksheet for compiling information.)

What Should You Keep— and for How Long?

Once you've finished filing your return, the next consideration is how long to keep the material you've collected. The simple answer is to keep whatever you need to persuade the IRS that everything on your return is accurate. Hang on to the evidence for as long as the IRS has the right to question your return.

Ordinarily, that's three years from the due date for the return, including extensions, to assess any additional tax. But a return can be audited for six years if the IRS suspects the taxpayer has neglected to report substantial income; if fraud is suspected, there is no time limit.

Your recordkeeping system doesn't have to be elaborate or sophisticated. What is more important is to have a system—and the discipline to keep the files up to date.

- **Set up a separate Reference File** for each year's tax information, and separate it into folders for each item-ized deduction: medical, taxes, interest, etc. Save any bills, receipts and canceled checks that correspond to those deductions.
- **If you write off the cost of a business car,** keep the logbook in which you recorded your trips as well as evidence of the costs you incur.
- **If you claim as a dependent** someone who is not your

ORGANIZING FOR THE TAXMAN

Regardless of your style, there are certain steps that are crucial:

- If you have a tax adviser, make an appointment to get together well before April 15 to determine exactly what records you need to keep if it is not clear to you. This will eliminate unnecessary paper, and insure that you retain essential information.

- Designate a place to keep any information relevant to your tax return. It can be a dresser drawer, a file cabinet, a shoebox, a calendar, a computer—in short, anything that works for you.

- Pay tax-deductible items by check or credit card whenever possible. At the end of the year, sorting canceled checks and credit card receipts is much easier than sorting cash-register receipts with blurred dates and miscellaneous unidentified scraps of paper. Some banks and brokerage firms even offer systems that break out taxable items paid by check. Computer software programs, including *TaxCut*, which includes tax tips from the editors of *Kiplinger's Personal Finance* magazine (www.kiplinger.com), are also available for that purpose.

- Ask yourself how much of your record-keeping or tax preparation you really need or want to do yourself. Is there someone who can help—another family member, perhaps, or a professional?

child, keep a separate file for the evidence that shows you provide more than half of that person's support.

- **Keep information** that relates to the purchase of a house at least six years after the sale of the house. This includes your title, deed of purchase, information about your home's purchase price and the cost of major capital improvements.

- **Records that verify the amount you paid** for an investment (your cost basis) should be kept for three years after you've sold the investment and reported your gains or losses on your tax return.

- **Keep the tax returns** themselves forever.

- **Remember, you may want some records,** such as warranties for major purchases, beyond the time the IRS requires for audit purposes.

Your To-Read Pile

Your to-read pile may be one of your biggest challenges. Most of us find it tough to stay current with all the newspapers, magazines and books we want to read. Add professional journals and newsletters, instruction guides for the electronic gadgets we've got in the house, and promotional materials for insurance policies, self-improvement opportunities and political candidates. The task of keeping up with our reading becomes overwhelming.

In many cases, the real issue is not *to read*, but *to remember*. We want to be well-balanced in our knowledge so our lives will be more productive. We also feel we should read broadly because we worry we might miss something that could be important to our lives, or at least be a lot of fun! And we'd like to be well-read to make a good impression on friends and colleagues.

There's a very positive aspect to an overflowing to-read pile. It shows that we have many interests, which makes us interesting, creative people. Remember that a creative mind always has more ideas than the body can carry out. Many of those ideas come from what we read, but what we must remember is that there's no shortage of resources for ideas. There will always be more things to read, so spend your time reading, not feeling guilty over what you haven't read.

Be Selective

The first step in solving the problem is to accept the fact that it's unlikely you will ever be able to read all

EFFECTIVE CATALOG SHOPPING

Write the name and page number of the items you're interested in on the catalog. When you're ready to order, you'll be able to find the items quickly. Or tear out the pages—but be sure to jot down the phone number you'll need for ordering or tear out the mail order form—and throw the rest of the catalog away.

the things you think you ought to read, let alone all the things you would like to read—even if you do take the best speed-reading course the country has to offer. The law of rising expectations will undoubtedly prevail: If you increase the speed at which you can read, the amount of information you want to read will also increase. So, although completing a speed-reading course may be a desirable goal, it will not solve the problem of the ever-growing to-read pile.

The issue is not reading faster, but reading smarter. One of the first rules is to be more selective. Instead of taking time browsing through a magazine or journal, check the table of contents for articles that relate to your specific interest. Read lead paragraphs, lead sentences and closing paragraphs to get the main idea. Beware of the lures of modern day marketing: Do you catch yourself reading a publication or major advertising promotion just because the promoter made it look so appealing, while at the same time ignoring a publication you must read to be current in your field?

Play a game with yourself to see how much potential reading material you can eliminate before it ever gets to your to-read pile. How much can go directly into the wastebasket, for example. Or, if you can't resist the temptation to read everything that comes into your house—even if you have no need to read it—take yourself off mailing and circulation lists (see the box on page 35). Also, be particularly leery of those publications you receive as business perks. Ask yourself, "If I were paying for this publication out of my own pocket, would I still order?" If not, cancel the subscription, or give it to someone who would benefit more from reading the publication.

Make an inventory of the magazines and periodicals you receive each month. Estimate the amount of time it would take to read them the way you'd like to. Are your expectations realistic? If not, what can you do about it? Identify which publications contribute the most value. Consider alternating subscriptions every year or two.

Improve Your Technique

When you have eliminated absolutely everything you think you can, try to improve your reading techniques.

Perfectionism is one stumbling block in reducing the to-read pile. For example, you receive an alumni newsletter in the mail. You're interested in the news of your former classmates, but there simply isn't time to read it now. So you put the newsletter on the credenza behind your desk or in the basket beside your lounge chair in the family room. Guess what? Six months later it's still there—along with the next five issues!

Or you receive a journal from your professional association. You feel obligated to keep up with the latest happenings, and there are some activities in which you would like to participate, but there's no time to read the journal when it arrives. Into the basket it goes. By the time you get around to reading it a month later, the seminar that really suited your needs is filled or already over.

The end result in both of these cases is usually that you eventually tire of seeing the piles and toss everything out. No purpose is served in holding on to them except to create clutter and guarantee guilt.

There are no magic words to make your to-read pile disappear if it's too high. You have three options: Read it, file it or throw it away. If you choose the first option, you face a time-management problem. There is only one way to read, and that is to create the time to do it.

Make an appointment with yourself to read and mark it on your calendar, just as you would make an appointment with someone else to go to the movies. Con-

Perfectionism is one stumbling block in reducing the to-read pile.

Sometimes the best way to use a few unexpected moments is to do some deep breathing or fantasize about a day at the beach!

sider your own biological rhythms. Is it easier to get up an hour earlier or stay up an hour later? Can you take your lunch to work two days a week and read through your lunch hour? To stay abreast with your business reading, can you set aside a quiet time each day, or two to three times a week, when your assistant will screen out all but the most important calls? Or can you put your phone on voice mail?

Incorporate

Look for creative ways to incorporate reading into your daily life. Instead of driving to work, can you use public transportation or a car pool and use that time for reading? Do you travel frequently? If so, designate a place to put reading materials you can take with you on your next trip. Then use those inevitable delays as a gift-of-reading time instead of a total disaster.

Do you drive a car pool for your children and end up waiting for them, spend time waiting in doctor's offices or go to meetings that frequently begin late? Always carry reading materials with you so you can make the time productive.

I'm not suggesting that every uncommitted moment should be spent reading—or anything else. Sometimes the best way to use a few unexpected moments is to do some deep breathing or fantasize about a day at the beach! However, if you carry reading material with you, you can make a conscious choice instead of finding yourself in an unconscious trap. Keep in mind that it can be fun reading. One client of mine loves to read spy novels. He always carries one with him on airplanes—the only time he enjoys that relaxation luxury.

Categorize Your Reading

Separate your reading into types of reading. Keep all high priority reading together so that when you have set aside reading time you won't be tempted by material that belongs in a lower priority category.

Put material from other categories where it can be

read as time permits. For example, many people enjoy reading mail-order catalogs when they want to relax. If you do, put a basket beside your bed where you can collect the catalogs, and read them at your leisure. (Note on the front cover the page number for items of interest.) But when the basket gets full, that's your signal it's time to toss some out—or start over completely.

"PACKRATTING" COSTS

One of my clients used to have all kinds of books, magazines and newspapers all over her house until she built a new house and discovered what it cost her per square foot. When she saw what her packrat behavior was costing her, she threw all the reading material out! Remember, this country is full of libraries!

Another category might be materials that you would like to read but that are not a high priority and will be outdated at a specific time. Jot down on the cover the deadline date for reading. If you haven't read it in, say, six weeks, or when the basket is full, throw the material out. This category of reading is a good one to carry with you when you're traveling. As you finish reading something, you can toss it, offering the added incentive of lightening your luggage!

Put the category of reading in a location where you are most likely to read it. For example, I like to read catalogs when I'm watching television, so I put it in a basket beside my chair. I do high-priority reading when I travel, so I carry it in an Action File in my briefcase.

"Just in Time" Reading

Many people are hesitant to file away an article that they haven't read because they're afraid it may not be worth it. My experience has made it clear that we are more apt to read immediately those articles that relate to important or timely issues. For example, if you find an article on planning a birthday party for a five-year-old and your son just turned four, your motivation to read the article will not be very great, but if his fifth birthday is a month away you will be very interested in the information.

When you find an article that interests you but you don't have time to read it, tear it out, file it according to the topic it relates to and discard the magazine. Then, when you are dealing with the topic, it will be much easier to determine if the article is useful. If the article re-

TOO MANY UNREAD PAPERS

A friend was constantly irritated by the pile of daily
newspapers that she did not get to over the course of
the week. It added stress and a sense of obligation to
the point where she felt forced to read a week's worth
of papers on Saturday because she paid for them.
The problem was quickly eliminated when she amended
her subscription to receive only the weekend papers.

mains in the magazine in the pile of magazines behind
your credenza, it's highly unlikely you'll remember it, let
alone have the time to go through the pile to find it!

If you frequently need to save articles related to
your personal or professional interests, consider creating
a separate file system that I call a Library File. To determine where information should go, use the same question you ask for your Reference Files: "What word will I
think of if I want to find this information?" For example,
an article about how to choose a caterer could go in a Library File called Entertaining, or an article on antique
restorers could go in Decorating or House Information.

Always read with a pen in your hand. If you find a
magazine article you'd like to save but can't tear it out
because your spouse hasn't read the issue or there is another article of interest on the other side, just note the
page number of the article (and the subject, if you wish)
on the cover. Later on, when you're faced with stacks of
old magazines, you will be able to identify quickly which
contain articles you want to keep. (You may also discover
that some articles interest you less than they did when
you marked them.)

Set Limits

One of the most common questions from clients is
"How long should I keep books, newspapers and
magazines?" There is no right or wrong answer. It depends entirely upon your feelings about these publications. For example, some people enjoy being around

books, whether they have read them or not—or ever intend to read them. They appreciate books the way other people appreciate art. If you feel that way and you have enough bookshelf space, by all means keep them.

However, if you're like me and too many books create stress, eliminate those you've read and don't intend to read again and those either given to you (even if they did cost a fortune) or that you picked up off the "Under $2.00" shelf in the local bookstore and that you never expect to read. But don't just throw them away! There are many productive uses for unwanted books, as discussed later in this chapter. As for the books you still want to read, make an appointment with yourself and get to it.

What about magazines and newspapers? Look at each publication individually, and make a decision about how long you will keep it. For example, if you have young children, you may feel compelled to keep your National Geographic magazines as reference material for future school projects. If you really enjoy cooking or you entertain frequently, you may decide to keep *Gourmet* permanently. News magazines, however, are of little value when they are more than a week or two old, unless you happen to be a historian or a journalist.

I use the Sunday paper as my signal that it's time to discard the previous week's papers. If there are articles I really want to read but did not get around to it, I tear them from the paper and file them in my Reference File, as discussed earlier in this chapter. Consider photocopying newspaper articles. They can be reduced in size and therefore take up less file space. In addition, the photocopy will last longer than a newspaper copy.

Identify those items that are of extremely limited value when they become outdated. Last week's *TV Guide*, old phone books, catalogs from stores from which you've never ordered, and last month's *Newsweek* are primary candidates for the trash.

If you really enjoy holding on to publications, what is the best way to do it? The first step is the same one we use in organizing so many things: Put like objects together. For example, keep all travel books together, all kitchen magazines together, all catalogs together. If you

Look at each publication individually and make a decision about how long you will keep it.

SELECTIVITY SAVES TIME

A client of mine who is a physician scans the table of contents of his medical journals as they arrive, notes which articles he wants filed and jots in the margin the name of the file where they should be filed. His assistant files the articles so they are available for his reading when he is dealing with a particular medical problem.

like, put colored dots on book bindings to make it easy to keep them in the appropriate category. Put magazines in cardboard or plastic magazine holders—labeled with the name and year of publication. When you see the amount of one category you have accumulated, you can determine whether you really want to take up that much of your living space with that item.

When you get rid of material that has proved helpful, consider putting the bibliographic information in a file on the subject or inside another publication you keep on the subject. If you use the *Taming the Paper Tiger* software, you will find the deleted items or archive function to be a handy tool to keep track of these discarded materials.

After you've categorized all your reading material and eliminated anything that you decide is excess, the final step is to designate a place to keep what remains. To determine that, ask yourself where you would be most likely to read or otherwise utilize the information. If it is reference material, in what room would you look for it? Travel and foreign-language books might be best in the library or family room, while light fare such as *People* or *Reader's Digest* might go in a basket beside your lounge chair to read during commercials. Millions of us enjoy reading in the bathroom, so a magazine rack hanging on the back of the bathroom door might be the perfect place for the lightweight reading.

Alternative Measures

If bookshelf space is a problem even after you have eliminated all the publications you can, then what? If you have some books that are important to the family but not particularly to you, identify your alternatives. Is there someone else in the family who would enjoy them more? If your children want them but are not in a position to take them now, put them in boxes in a safe, but less accessible location in your home—clearly labeled. If there is no available space, consider renting a self-storage unit.

If you have books that no longer interest you or your family, donate them to a library or professional association, or sell them at a secondhand bookstore. If you have a large number of books, check your phonebook commercial listings to find a book dealer who will pick up the books at your house, so you can avoid the hassle of carting them around.

Consider alternatives to reading. There is nothing that says you are un-American if you don't read the daily newspaper. A friend of mine says it took him years to admit that he really could read all he wanted to of the newspaper by looking over the shoulder of the person standing next to him on the subway. Instead of reading the paper, consider watching a half-hour nightly news broadcast at least a few times a week.

Another way to keep up with books that you'd like to read is to buy—or rent or borrow—the audiotape version. Books on tape are a great way to relax or to educate yourself while commuting. I regularly listen to these tapes on a cassette player that plugs into my car's CD player. In addition, I carry a small portable tape recorder so if I hear something that I want to act on or make a note of I can record it. (I can also use the tape to make an oral note of something I think about as I'm driving.) When I reach my destination, I transfer my recorded notes to my calendar, to-do list, rotary telephone file, Reference Files or other appropriate place. Taping parts of tapes is like saving articles of interest from a magazine instead of keeping the whole issue. In this instance, I avoid creating a tape pile.

If you have books that no longer interest you or your family, donate them to a library or professional association, or sell them at a secondhand bookstore.

Your To-Write Pile

I f you want to see guilt written on the faces of a lot of people in a big hurry, just mention the phrase "letter writing!" The mobility of our society and our changing lifestyles have created an enormous network of people with whom we would like, or think we ought, to communicate. High divorce and remarriage rates result in larger, extended families. All of these situations have complicated our lives and made it more difficult than ever to keep up written communication. The advent of e-mail has made keeping in touch easier, but has also created a new system that needs organizing (see the box on page 116 for some ideas for managing e-mail).

Personal Correspondence

A s with every other aspect of paper management that we've discussed, selectivity is the key. There will always be more people to write to than you will have time for, so choose those who mean the most to you. Keep in mind that circumstances change, and we do outgrow friendships. At twenty-five, you probably felt that your college roommate would always be an important person in your life, but your paths led in different directions and you now realize you have little in common.

If you're serious about keeping up with your friends through letters instead of or in addition to e-mails, the most important thing to do is to set aside a regular time to write, such as one Sunday a month, or one letter before your favorite television show. Write just one letter a week and you can communicate with 52 friends each year.

A WORD ABOUT E-MAIL COMMUNICATION

For better or worse, e-mail is becoming a major form of written communication. Using it well can make the difference between gracious and annoying. Here are some suggestions:

Sending E-mail Your Recipients Will Love:

- **Use the subject line to describe the topic of your e-mail clearly.** This is helpful for the recipient, and for you if you want to find a message you've sent.
- **For a lengthy or complicated e-mail,** create the e-mail in your word processing program, then copy to your e-mail. If you have an e-mail glitch during the sending process, you can easily retrieve your message.
- **When replying to any e-mail, attach enough of the old message** for the recipient to remember the content of the original e-mail, but delete unnecessary information or duplication.
- **If you are sending the same message to muptiple recipients,** use the blind copy feature so you don't disclose other people's e-mail addresses.

- **Avoid sending e-mail attachments whenever possible.** Receivers are becoming more reluctant to open attachments due to the increasing prevalence of viruses.

Managing Your Incoming E-mail:

- **Whenever you open your incoming e-mail,** apply The FAT System (File-Act-Toss).
- **Apply the "2-Do Rule" whenever possible.** If you can reply in two minutes, then do it right away. It will take longer to file it and retrieve it again than to "just do it."
- **For e-mail that takes more time to reply,** either leave them in the in-box or file in an appropriate folder such as Action or Reply.
- **For e-mail you want to keep in electronic format,** create an electronic folder called Reference or file by subject, such as Family History.
- **If you need or want a paper copy of an e-mail for future reference,** print it out and file it in your paper-management system.

Do whatever you can to make letter writing enjoyable and efficient. If that means using a computer or a typewriter, by all means do so. Some of us would never write to our family and friends if we had to write by hand—and in the case of a few people I know the recipients wouldn't be able to read the letters if we did. Personally, I love letters—all letters—and I have yet to criticize someone who wrote me on their PC.

If you're going to write, choose stationery and a pen that you like and find easy to use. Select different styles of writing paper for different occasions. Carry notepaper in your handbag or briefcase so you can jot a quick note while you wait for an appointment. This is also a great way to use postcards that you pick up while on vacation.

Thank-you notes and letters of condolence are especially important kinds of correspondence. Not only do we want to do what is socially correct, but also we want people to know we appreciate their kindnesses and care about their suffering. In some cases you may find it's easier to make a telephone call than it is to write a letter. If you feel you must write, do whatever you can to simplify the process. I find it helpful to purchase multiple copies of any thank you or sympathy cards I particularly like. If you don't have a card on hand and don't have time to get one, write a note on personal stationery.

We often put off writing a letter because there are so many things we want to say. But the longer we put it off, the more there is to write. Then we decide we will wait until Christmas, but the holidays come and go, and the Christmas cards that we did manage to purchase are still in the desk drawer. Finally, we are so embarrassed by our negligence that we completely lose contact with a friend.

If you recognize this scenario, ask yourself when was the last time you got a short note from a friend and complained, "My, that sure was a short note!" A short note is better than no note at all. Beware of perfectionism. Write what you can when you can, and the people who are truly friends will understand and be glad to hear from you.

Birthdays and Anniversaries

There are a variety of ways to handle those annual special events. First, find a place to consistently list birthdays and anniversaries—a special-occasion book, a section of your to-do book, or on a card in your rotary phone-file. (If you keep track of many dates, create one card for each month.)

Next you've got to find a way to remind yourself to look at the list. One person I know checks her list at the beginning of each month and transfers into her calendar the days she needs to mail the cards or gifts (not the day

> Beware of perfectionism. Write what you can when you can, and the people who are truly friends will understand and be glad to hear from you.

of the birthday, when it is usually too late to take action). You may prefer to put all the reminders into your calendar at once for the entire year.

Personal Information Managers will do this for you—just enter the dates and have a tickler or reminder pop up before the event. Enter "birthday reminders" into your favorite search engine to find a variety of on-line reminder services.

One of the risks of purchasing greeting cards that you see and like, even if you don't know to whom you will send them, is forgetting you have them—or not being able to find them at the right time. To avoid this, establish a specific place to keep the cards. Be sure that it is easily accessible if you want to encourage yourself to use them. If you keep more than a dozen cards on hand, organizing them by occasion will save you time and prevent frustration. Buy one of those beautiful cardboard boxes, or use large envelopes (8½" x 11"), tuck in the flap to make a large pocket envelope, and write Anniversary, Birthday, etc. on the outside. Arrange the envelopes alphabetically, and put them in your Reference File.

Business Versus Pleasure

Again, it is very helpful to have stationery on hand that you can use for writing or typing business letters. You can often answer a business letter by writing a note on the letter itself. (Keep a copy for yourself only if necessary, rather than out of habit.) Another quick way to write a business letter is to use a personalized postcard. I had some printed to use for requesting information or confirming appointments.

Separate your to-write category into Business and Personal. You may feel in the mood to write a quick thank you note but not to inquire about a discrepancy in your credit card bill. Sometimes you may find it convenient, or even fun, to take a box of note stationery and your To Write—Personal Action File with you to the doctor's office or the beach.

Family Records

A father had to revaccinate his five-year-old for school because he couldn't find the child's immunization card and the doctor who treated her was no longer in practice. A business executive missed an important financial opportunity when she needed to fly to Italy but couldn't find her passport. A financially strapped widow lost more than $2,000 in medical insurance reimbursements because she didn't file the claims within the two-year time limit.

What if you need to make an overseas business trip or you want to sell some stock—could you find your passport or records of the stock's purchase easily? What if you or your spouse—or both of you—suddenly died or became incapacitated? Would someone know where to find your will or what insurance benefits you have? What about the key to your safe deposit box? Could anyone find the cash stashed away in a money-market fund? Make sure any information that your survivors need is easily accessible. If any of these questions makes you feel uneasy, organizing your records can bring great peace of mind. As you do, you will be able to identify areas that need attention, such as out-of-date wills, inadequate homeowner's insurance, missing legal documents, or a beneficiary change you need to make on your insurance policy. Chapter 10 explained how to organize and maintain Reference Files. This chapter suggests what material should go into the folders.

Bank Records

Your files should include the name and address of each

PROTECT IRREPLACEABLE DOCUMENTS

Keep papers that are difficult or impossible to replace in a safe deposit box or a fireproof box in your home. The box should be large enough to hold everything that should be in it—and small enough to keep out things that do not need to be there. Do not use the box as a catchall for souvenirs.

Keep in your Reference File at home a list of everything you have in your safe deposit box. Update the list as you add or remove items. If you store documents from investment properties or securities, the rental can be claimed as a deduction on your tax return.

Finally, make sure family members know where the box is located and where the key is kept.

---

bank, credit union, or savings and loan association where you have an account. Also include each type of account, the account numbers and signers of the accounts, as well as numbers of CDs and the location of passbooks, statements and CDs.

Credit Cards and Charge Accounts

List account numbers and names of issuers so that lost or stolen cards can be promptly reported missing. In the event of death, survivors can notify issuers of the cards and inform banks if accounts are to be closed or listed in a different name.

Tax Records

Be sure that family members know where to locate information for filing income tax returns and where you keep records from previous years. Chapter 14 has detailed information on this subject.

Investment Records

While the monetary rewards resulting from investments can create a great sense of security, for many people the paper generated by those investments often creates a great sense of insecurity. One of my clients had a four-drawer filing cabinet filled with annual reports dating back more than a decade. She had never read any, but she was convinced she should keep them—just in case!

Investment companies send many different kinds

of information. Some can be thrown out immediately; some need to be kept until you've made a decision on the information; some material needs to be kept as long as you keep a particular security. For example, investment companies regularly send material intended to inform you of their recommendations for stock purchases. If you decide not to buy the stock, you don't need to keep the recommendation. But if you do act on the information, you'll need to keep the subsequent records of the purchase, along with statements that show how much the investment appreciates or depreciates so you'll have an accurate record when you eventually sell the stock and have to figure your tax on the transaction.

Keep a separate file for essential information, including your monthly statements and the confirmations of your various transactions, as opposed to the generic information that is sent to all investors. Here's an outline of the kind of information you should have in your files:

STOCKS, BONDS AND MUTUAL FUNDS. Where are the certificates kept? (The safest option is to have your

EMERGENCY DOCUMENTS KIT

It's a good idea to keep an easy-to-grab, resealable plastic bag or container in case you have to leave your home quickly in an emergency. Contents could include:

- **traveler's checks and cash,** including change for phone calls (or keep your cell phone nearby);
- **list of banks** and other financial institutions you use;
- **videotape** of everything of value in your home;
- **photocopies of deeds** to property—or any records that would be difficult to replace; and
- **copies of important medical** and eyeglass/contact lens information.

Also refer to chapter 12 for tips for dealing with emergencies and disaster-proofing your papers.

HELP FOR LOCATING YOUR DOCUMENTS

Your Family Records Organizer is a CD-ROM developed by Kiplinger (www.kiplinger.com/organizer, 800-280-7165, Operator 89) that offers a convenient means of recording where you keep all of your important documents and listing names and numbers of key contact people. *Taming the Paper Tiger* software www.thepapertiger.com) can also be used to inventory this essential information, and will automatically print an index that can be shared with all the people who should have access.

broker hold all your stock certificates.) List the names and addresses of brokers, list of holdings, including owner's name, date bought and purchase price for each security.

KEOGH, IRA, 401(K) PLANS. For each family member, include name of institution and location of papers, if they are at some other location, such as our office or your lawyer's.

OTHER INVESTMENTS. For collectibles, what kind do you have? Where are they kept? Who should appraise them for sale or insurance purposes?

IF YOU OWN A BUSINESS, WHAT TYPE IS IT? Where is it located? Where do you keep important documents relating to it (in a safe at the business, or your safe deposit box, for example)? Who should be contacted if there's a problem?

If you own real estate, note who else owns the property if it is held jointly. This includes property owned jointly by married persons. If the joint owner is not a spouse, give the name, address, and interest of each joint owner. Include the name and address of the mortgagee, how the property is titled, the date of acquisition and cost, mortgage terms (including the original amount), the monthly payment and the payment-due date, and date of final payment.

Retirement Income Records

In planning ahead for retirement, it is extremely important for you and your spouse to have a complete up-to-date record of your pension plan or plans, any annuities you will receive, rents or royalties and your estimated social security benefits. The Social Security Administration sends an annual statement of benefits to everyone age 25 and over. You can also obtain a statement of your social security earnings by sending a Request for Statement of Earnings form to the Social Security Administration. These forms are available from your local office.

In most families, one person handles most of the financial matters. If you've been the family controller, you know the intricacies of the situation. Continuity in planning and implementing financial strategies is important, and while you can't expect someone else to follow your exact track, you want your successor to understand what you have been doing. This means that in addition to listing where the assets are, you should provide information on managing any complicated situations to help your successor take charge of your affairs.

Trusts

List any trusts you have created or trusts created by others under which you possess any power, beneficial interest or trusteeship. Include the name of the trust, location, trustee and beneficiary.

Wills

For couples, the importance of both parties having up-to-date wills cannot be overemphasized. The individual who makes no will forfeits any assurance that his or her property will be distributed according to his or her wishes, and will probably cause unnecessary difficulties and possible financial losses for the survivors. When a person dies without a will, the distribution of the estate is governed by state laws that may not fit the best interest of the family.

Review your will periodically. You'll need to update it

NEED AN EMERGENCY BANK ACCOUNT?

Many banks block joint accounts when they receive notification of death of one of the joint owners. If this is the case, each spouse may wish to set up a separate emergency account in his or her own name. Ask your bank to write you a letter stating its policy, so you know beforehand.

if you have married, divorced or remarried, if heirs have been born or died, if the size or nature of your estate has changed, or if you have moved to a different state.

Liabilities Record

There are two primary reasons for keeping a complete liabilities record. First, should you become ill and require hospitalization, your family should know not only to whom you owe money, but also when payments are due to avoid unnecessary complications. Second, should you die, a comprehensive record of your liabilities serves as a basis to dismiss any false claims made against your estate.

Include installment debts on homes, automobiles, credit cards, home improvements, personal loans, furniture, appliances and business loans. Information needed includes current balances, monthly payments, due dates, and whether there is debt insurance.

Insurance Records

The information about your policies is important for two reasons. In the event of your death, it ensures that your family and executor of your estate will know what insurance benefits are available, which companies and insurance agents to contact and how to file claims. In addition, should you become incapacitated due to accident or illness your family will be able to pay policy premiums to keep your coverage in force.

Keep automobile and homeowners insurance policies in your Reference Files so you can refer to them quickly to update or check coverage.

Also keep medical insurance policies in your Reference Files because you will need to refer to them when making claims. The simplest, most effective way to keep track of the status of claims is to create three Action Files. Every insurance claim falls into one of these stages, so it's simple to check on the status of any claim as it moves through the system.

Label the first Medical Insurance—To Be Submitted. This contains the blank claim forms, the instructions on how to submit a claim and any receipts from the doctor, laboratory, clinic or pharmacy. Label the second file folder Medical Insurance—Submitted, But Not Paid. This contains a photocopy of the patient copy of any claims you submitted for reimbursement but for which you have not yet received payment. Finally, the third folder should be labeled Medical Claims—Paid. If you are able to take any medical deduction on your tax return, keep this information for three years after the filing year.

> ### WILL-SIGNING SAVVY
>
> Have an extra witness observe the signing, even more than the law requires. If your will is ever probated, one or more of your witnesses may have moved away or died. Use witnesses you know personally so that they can be easily located.

Keep life insurance policies in your safe deposit box, but keep information in your Reference Files identifying the name of the company for each policy, the policy number, face amount, beneficiaries, whether there has been a loan taken on the policy, premium due date, and the agent's name.

Medical Records

In addition to insurance records, it is important to keep individual medical records. The simplest method is to establish a separate Reference File for each family member (Medical—Mary and Medical—John, for example). Include doctor and dental receipts that identify diseases and treatments. (These can be culled from the Health Insurance—Paid file). Also note in these files information about blood type, eyeglass prescriptions and allergies.

Finally, many people like to keep articles about medical developments or pamphlets they pick up at the doctor's office or the pharmacy. Do not include this information in your medical records file. Make a separate

MARK YOUR HOUSEHOLD POSSESSIONS

As you take inventory, mark your property with some identification. Your police department may have a special identification program. You can also purchase engravers to mark items with a code you think up.

file for these informational materials (for example, Medical Information—Coronary Care).

Survivor's Benefits Records

Tragically, many survivor's benefits are left unclaimed because the survivors are unaware of their existence. These benefits are not paid automatically. Applications must be made on prescribed forms and specific documents furnished.

The most well-known benefit is social security. Survivors of deceased veterans or active-duty service personnel are also eligible for benefits through the Veterans Administration. These benefits do not conflict with claims made under social security, but again, they are not paid automatically. In most cases, claims must be made within two years following death.

There are several other possible sources of survivor's benefits, including Worker's Compensation, employer's group insurance policy, individual life insurance policy, health/accident policy, auto/casualty insurance, and group policies through trade unions or fraternal organizations.

Keep all relevant policies, addresses, phone numbers and contact names in your Reference Files, and be sure your family is aware of these benefits and where the information is filed.

In Case of Ill or Aging Family Members

This is one of the most difficult areas of paper management, but it's also one of the most important. Make sure your own records are in order and that someone knows where you keep them. In addition, be sure you or another family member possesses or has access to the information for any family members for whom you or they are responsible.

You will need a durable power of attorney if that person dies or becomes unable to make his or her own decisions. In addition to dealing with matters necessary in the event of death, changes in records also need to be made for automobile titles, stocks and bonds, bank accounts, etc.

Here's one more very important thing to consider: Be sure to include any special instructions to the family about your memorial service, funeral or burial preferences. It will be a big comfort. A friend of mine said she felt bad when her mother died because she did not know whether she wanted her wedding ring left on when she was buried.

Family-History Records

The purpose of this category is to assemble in one place important family information that might be necessary to obtain a passport, apply for social security and veterans benefits or to file a loan application. For each family member include birth date (copy of birth certificate if available; original should be in a safe deposit box), social security number, and a copy of any marriage or divorce certificate. Also keep here any family genealogy records.

Include in this Reference File the names and telephone numbers of your accountant, financial planner, employee-benefits adviser, insurance agents (life, health, car, personal property, homeowners), stockbroker, or other financial adviser.

Education, Employment and Military Records

Keep a separate file for each family member. For example, Education Records—Paul and Military Records—Bob. The information in these files simplifies the task of writing or rewriting a resume, applying for admission to an educational institution, or applying for a new job.

Household Inventory

One of the most neglected family records is the household inventory. If there is a fire or burglary in your home, this record will help you remember what has to

In case of a fire or burglary, a household inventory will help you remember what has to be replaced and determine the value of each item.

IN CASE OF DEATH . . .

You may not like to think about such things, but by planning ahead, some of the stress involved when a family member dies can be limited. Here are some lists of information someone in the family should have, or have access to.

To get a burial permit:
- Name of the deceased, home address, telephone number
- How long in state
- Occupation and title
- Name, address and phone number of business
- Social Security number
- Armed services serial number
- Date and place of birth
- Citizenship
- Father's name and birthplace
- Mother's name and birthplace

Documents:
- Deeds to property, automobile titles
- Insurance policies
- Income-tax returns
- Military-discharge papers
- Disability claims

- Birth certificate or other legal proof of age
- Citizenship papers, if naturalized
- Will
- Social Security card
- Death certificate (certificates for burial permit)
- Bank books
- Marriage and divorce certificates, if any

To Notify:
- Doctor of health maintenance organization
- Funeral director of memorial society
- Institution to which remains may be donated if living will exists
- Memorial park
- Relatives, friends, employers of deceased
- Insurance agents
- Attorney, accountant or executor of estate
- Religious, fraternal, civic, veterans' groups
- Newspaper regarding death notice

be replaced and determine the value of each item. An inventory is also an excellent way to make certain that your insurance protection is sufficient. One client of mine purchased a $15,000 painting but neglected to add it to his insurance policy. When someone accidentally damaged the painting, the owner had to pay for repairs himself.

When you make an inventory, start at one point in the room and go all the way around, listing everything. The more complete the information, the more valuable it will be. Include information such as initial cost, model numbers, brand names and descriptions. Take photographs of the room and special items so that identifying or replacing them will be easier. Videotapes make excellent inventories. Be sure to include the basement, garage and attic. Estimate the replacement cost for each item and add up the total to determine how much insurance you should have.

Update your inventory every six months or so by adding recent purchases and adjusting replacement costs. Some insurance policies automatically increase replacement costs. Be sure you know the limits in your homeowner's policy with regard to valuables such as jewelry, furs and art.

If you find the task of preparing a household inventory overwhelming, check your classified phone book listings and find a professional to do it, such as Asset Verification Inc. (www.assetverification.com), who offer special pricing to readers of this book. Or get other members of the family to help you. Keep the records in a fireproof safe at home or your safe deposit box.

Warranties and Instructions

Gadgets have become both the joy and the frustration of modern life. It is a joy when you can find what you need when you need it, but it's a major frustration when you can't remember how to operate it—and you can't find the instruction book!

Every time you purchase a new appliance, toy, tool, or other household item, you are blessed with several new pieces of paper: a consumer registration card; a promotion brochure for other products from the same manufacturer; an instruction booklet; and, frequently, a consumer questionnaire. To further complicate matters, often a company will issue the same warranty for several products. Just because you can find a warranty doesn't mean you will know what it protects.

There are several steps you can take to minimize this problem:

■ **Decide where you will keep all warranty and instructional information.** I don't recommend separating them because often one piece of paper will have the warranty and the instruction. You may decide to keep those related to kitchen appliances in the kitchen so they will be readily available, or if your kitchen storage space is limited, you may choose to put them in the household Reference File under Warranties and Instructions. It's also helpful to put the instruction booklet with the stereo, telephone or tape recorder so you can refer to it easily. Keep instructions relating to clothing (if they are not attached) in a plastic bag in the laundry room. Write the name of the item—such as blue comforter—on the instructions.

- **Keep the receipt with the warranty.** Whenever you make a purchase, staple the receipt to the warranty information so you can easily prove date of purchase, or put the date on the front of the warranty for your own information.

- **Decide now whether you will or will not fill out consumer information cards and warranty registration cards.** We often take longer shuffling the card than it would take to fill it out! The manufacturer doesn't require that you complete the cards to make the warranty valid, but it is essential if you need to be reached for product recall.

Family Memorabilia and Photographs

I t's September. The summer vacations, family gatherings and neighborhood barbecues were great fun. All that remain are warm memories, 37 envelopes of photographs and 13 videotapes that pop up like mushrooms all over the house but are nowhere to be found when you want to show them to someone! Add to that the boxes of old, unidentified family photographs your mother passed on to you for safekeeping, the trunk of family memorabilia you married along with your spouse, and the piles of creative clutter your children produce. There seems to be no relief in sight.

Feelings, Feelings

E motional involvement is the trickiest part of managing photographs and memorabilia. Even if we have no real interest in them, we feel that we should have some interest because they represent our family history. How do you know what your heritage will be while you are living it? We feel burdened because the memorabilia was so important to our parents or because it might be important to our yet unborn grandchildren. In the meantime, what do we do with all the stuff? It fills our attics and basements with boxes and our minds with guilt.

There are several steps you can take. First, recognize that is there no right or wrong approach. To decide what you want to do, begin gathering information about the alternatives you may have. Determine who else might be involved in the decision-making process.

It's not possible to foresee exactly how your descen-

You probably won't have the time to organize family memorabilia as perfectly as you'd like. Determine what you're willing and able to do, and do it.

dants will feel about this information. You can only make your decisions based on your current conditions and resources.

It Only *Seems* Hopeless

When you consider the amount of love, time and money that have gone into your memorabilia thus far you feel obligated to do something. The question is, "What?"

The simple baby books and photo albums like those our mothers used are no longer adequate for most families. Your intentions are good, but the mechanics of the task seem overwhelming—and even if you have the motivation, where do you find the time? How do you begin? What if you don't have the motivation? Can you risk ignoring the issue? And what about the space all this memorabilia takes in your house that you could be using for something else?

The most important step in dealing with the situation is to recognize that if left unchecked it is only going to get worse. As life goes on, the memorabilia simply accumulates. If the old stuff is out of control just think what another year's worth will be like!

Instead of wasting energy berating yourself every time you open the closet door and see those boxes of photographs, decide what action you can take to stop the cycle, and then do it. As with so many other aspects of paper management, the way to begin to make progress on this seemingly impossible task is to start with material you collect from today on. For the time being, ignore those piles of yesterday's memories. You can work on the backlog after you have devised a system that works for you.

Make It Easy on Yourself

Recognize that you probably won't have the time to organize family memorabilia as perfectly as you'd like. Determine what you're willing and able to do, and do it.

Design a system to fit your particular needs. Start by identifying an accessible place where you will put all the

EDITING AT THE STORE

One of my clients had a particularly difficult time dealing with her photographs. Keeping up with them was a continual frustration. She decided to come up with a system to correct it—one that fit her needs and circumstances—and that is exactly what she did.

She began by deciding not to bring photographs home until she had taken certain steps at her office, where she has her photos developed. First, she throws away any photographs that she does not like for whatever reason.

Next, she dates the photos and makes any necessary notations on them. (Note: Don't write directly on the photos—write first on an adhesive label, which you can then apply to the back of the picture.) She doesn't allow this step to become overwhelming, causing her to procrastinate about the project altogether. She has made a commitment to herself that the date is the only absolute requirement. (I would add names so years from now you'll know who's in the picture.)

Then she prepares a pile of heavy envelopes addressed to her parents and her in-laws. Her photo-processing store charges very little for duplicate prints, so she orders them automatically and sends selected duplicates to the relatives. (If you do not order duplicates but have some photos you want to duplicate, designate an envelope for those negatives that you need to return to the store for duplicating.) She immediately tosses whatever duplicates she does not send to her family and friends. This not only minimizes the number of photographs she has to deal with at home, but it pleases the grandparents immensely.

Finally, she puts the remaining photographs into the plastic pages the photo-processing store gives her when she pays for the pictures. All she has to do when she gets home is put the pages in a loose-leaf notebook.

An extra bonus resulting from her solution is that other members of her family have become much more interested in the photos because they are easily visible instead of buried in boxes in the closet.

She has since applied similar systems to other paper problems with success. She didn't think she had the discipline to do it, but she did. And you can, too.

memorabilia as you receive it or find it.

If you have a small amount, two boxes labeled Photographs and Memorabilia (napkins, brochures, invitations, matchbooks, dried flowers, etc.) may be all you'll need. If you have difficulty putting things away in their proper place, leave the lids off the boxes so they will be easier for you to use. At the end of the year, put the lids on the boxes, clearly label them (for example, Photos—

2002) and put them away. If you are short on storage space, put your boxes in an out-of-the-way location, such as the attic or basement. (Be careful not to store the boxes near a heat source or where it's moist. You don't want to go to the time and trouble of storing valued memories only to find them ruined.) Then note where they are on your Reference-File index (see Chapter 10).

SAVING FOR WHAT?

A friend of mine has a beautiful antique trunk in her family room. Inside it is filled with photographs—labeled with names and dates—but in no particular order. She sits on the floor with her grandchildren and shares her "treasure chest of memories." It is of no concern to her that the photos may be in less than perfect condition for future generations. She wants to enjoy them now!

Take whatever steps you can to make the organization process easier. If you don't have time to label each picture, make a note on the outside of the photo envelope as to the major categories, Summer—1997, or Jerry's Birthday Party—2001, for example. Some cameras will date the photos for you, or you might also have your photos developed at a lab that dates the back of your photos. (However, remember that the lab's date indicates when the film is developed, not when you took the pictures. Put a date on memorabilia, such as travel brochures, napkins, etc., as you receive it.

You will be able to re-create the occasion more easily if you decide to organize the materials in a more sophisticated style.

If you are a "memoraholic," you may need to divide your treasures into smaller categories to make them more manageable. There are several ways to do that. For example, if you have more than one child, you may want to have a photo album or memorabilia box for each one. Or you may want to create categories by type, such as Children's Art, Playbills, or Trips. These can be further broken down by destination and date, such as Europe—1997.

Get Kids Involved, Too

If you have children who are old enough to be involved in the decision making, ask them how they feel about the issue. You can give family memorabilia to your children, but be sure to do so with no strings attached. Let

MEMORABILIA SCRAPBOOKS

Memorabilia scrapbooks for special mementos other than photographs require a great deal of patience and creativity because many of them come in odd shapes and sizes. If you enjoy such projects you can have a ball, but if you don't it's probably unrealistic to expect much success at doing it. I recommend just leaving the items in your Memorabilia box.

them decide what to do with it based on their own needs and perspectives. If you feel strongly about what should happen to a particular keepsake and you would be hurt if your children didn't follow your wishes, keep it yourself—or find someone who agrees with your wishes.

Perhaps you've got material that's not important to you or your children. Ask a professional buyer of memorabilia if what you've got has any particular value to other people. If it does, perhaps you can give it to a charity, or sell it to a collector.

If you or your children feel it's important to go through everything yourselves to determine what you should keep, you'll need to develop a system for doing that. When time is a major factor, you may find it necessary or desirable to hire a professional organizing consultant to help you. If your children think it should be done, get a commitment from them as to how and when they will help.

Going It Alone

So you're going to fly solo through this project? Then you'll need a plan for accomplishing the task. Will you have to do it in bits and pieces or is it possible to spend several days working on the project? In either event, set goals for yourself. When you are having guests for dinner after work you can fix dinner in an hour if you need to, but if you have all day Saturday you can spend hours preparing dinner. This project works the same way. The more time you allow, the more it will take.

If your home has plenty of storage space your decisions about what to keep may be different from someone who lives in a small apartment. Off-site storage is a possibility if you have no space in your home. Be sure to compare prices when choosing one, and decide whether it's important to store the belongings close by or whether you can use a storage facility some distance away, which may save you money.

If you're having trouble parting with some items but don't have enough space, try to find ways of using memorabilia in your home or office. Thanks to the help of a creative friend, I now enjoy decorating with many memorabilia treasures that used to be buried in drawers, taking up room and never seen or enjoyed.

The Knack of Good Photo-Albuming

If you have taken all, or even some, of the steps described thus far, don't be surprised if one day you discover you really are ready to get those photographs into albums. It's a terrific project when you're housebound for one reason or another. Take whatever steps you can to get into the right frame of mind. Look on the process as a wonderful adventure into memory land. Get into comfortable clothes, put on your favorite music, fix a pot of coffee (but don't put it where you risk ruining any photographs if it spills!), and you're on your way. Take the following steps:

1. CHOOSE A GOOD PLACE TO WORK. Work in a comfortable chair at a large, clean, flat surface in an area where there's plenty of light and where you can leave the project until it is completed—or at least long enough to make some major progress. Resist the urge to rush out and buy photo albums at this point. Time will give you a better idea of the kind and quantity you need.

2. SORT THROUGH THE PHOTOS. Eliminate all those unsuccessful shots. Don't be discouraged—even professional photographers use only a small percentage of the

SLIDES, FILMS AND TAPES

Label slides in pen directly on the cardboard frame. Write so that you can look at the slide with the naked eye and read the label at the same time. This will be a big advantage should you ever want to put together a slide show.

Movies and videotapes should be organized, too. The key is to label them clearly. Keep peel-off labels and a felt-tipped pen in the same drawer or shelf as you keep your photographic equipment. Label as you go—even if you don't have time to do it perfectly.

photos they take. The first candidates for the wastebasket are double exposures and those fascinating shots of the inside of your lens cap. Very close behind are pictures you wish had been double exposures—like the one that shows only the lower half of your body—and those shots you wonder why you took (the one of the Christmas tree after you took down the decorations).

3. GIVE AWAY PHOTOS YOU WON'T USE. Many photos have little meaning to you, but could be special to someone else. They are fun to drop in the mail, and you'll undoubtedly bring a smile to Aunt Amanda's face!

4. IDENTIFY THE NEGATIVES. Before you separate the pictures from their negatives, write a description on the outside of the packet, such as Graduation—John, 2000, or simply use dates, and put the negatives in the packet. You may decide that once you have the picture and as many copies as you want you can throw the negatives away. If you want an insurance policy against unexpected disasters such as theft, fire or other loss (or divorce), keep the negatives in a separate place. Perhaps you could exchange negatives with a family member—or put negatives of favorite shots in your safe deposit box.

5. IDENTIFY THE PHOTOS. Determine where you are going to put the information about the photo. Don't

A SPECIAL GIFT FOR GRANDPARENTS

The next time a grandparent or other elderly family member is celebrating a birthday or other special occasion and you can't think of a suitable present, ask if they have any old photographs. Chances are they will, and nothing would please them more than to have your help in putting them in albums.

My grandmother talked for years about all the photographs she had never labeled. She was concerned that she couldn't remember everything about the pictures and that her handwriting was not good enough for future generations. I invited her to tell me about the photos while I made notes. Eventually I found at least one picture of every member in both grandparent's families. Whenever anyone comes to visit, it takes her only a few minutes to find the photo album. And the reminiscing begins.

It's still not clear who received the greatest gift.

write directly on the back of a photo—write first on an adhesive label, which you can then apply to the picture. Or use a separate piece of paper so that the information could be read after the photos are in albums. (Some energetic people do both.) The more information you record, the more joy the photo will bring in the years to come—who, what, where, when, and why. Experience has proven that, while a picture may be worth a thousand words, an unidentified picture is worth little to future generations.

6. CATEGORIZE THE PHOTOS. Sort photos into the categories you plan to use in the albums. Most people sort chronologically, but some do it by subject matter—for example, Family Reunions. CAUTION: Label the piles as you work. If you are interrupted, it won't take long to proceed with the sorting. One easy way to do this is to purchase inexpensive small baskets that can be labeled temporarily with removable labels.

7. SELECT ALBUMS. Now it's time to decide what kind of albums you want to use. A loose-leaf photograph album has a distinct advantage if you are trying to arrange photos chronologically because it's easy to add a page if you find more photos after you finish the project.

Make sure to use albums made of acid-free paper and polyester-based plastic if you want them available for future generations.

If you want to limit the number of albums you'll need, you may prefer the kind in which the photos are in individual sleeves, overlapping one another. The disadvantage of this type is that it will not accommodate over-sized photos.

8. INTO THE ALBUM THEY GO. Let your creativity loose! Enjoy experimenting with different arrangements. Feel free to trim photos to their best advantage. If you have several photos from one event, group them together on one or more pages and write a short scenario about the occasion, rather than labeling each photo individually.

"Scrapbooking" is a rapidly growing industry. Check your phone book's classified section for a shop in your area or www.creativememories.com to get the name of a consultant for classes in their home or yours, as well as tools and techniques you can use to creative beautiful albums that will preserve your photographs and other memorabilia.

Be Creative

As you browse through your photos, consider ways of using your favorites in some unusual way. Check with your local photographic-supply or film-processing shop for ideas. Here are some possibilities:

- **Make your own notecards or picture postcards.** Paste photos on plain note stationery slightly larger than your photo. Photo Talk stickers are available from a photographic-supply store. Use the stickers to add amusing comments above people's heads.

- **Make a photo T-shirt.** Take a color print that is the size you want to a copy shop that has a heat-transfer machine. Have a transfer made and applied to a T-shirt, or take the transfer home and apply it yourself, as you would an iron-on patch.

- **Make a jigsaw puzzle.** Companies advertise this service in the classified section of magazines, or check your local photo-finishing store. A great gift idea!

- **Make a poster.** Turn your pictures into artwork to hang in your family room or college dorm room. Consider panoramic views of places that are special to you. The same companies that make jigsaw puzzles can do this for you.

- **Make a calendar.** Custom photo-finishing labs are equipped to print a photo above a twelve-month calendar. This makes a great holiday gift idea for children, grandparents, friends or business associates.

- **Make a mousepad.** You can have your favorite photo to look at every time you use your computer.

- **Make a videotape from slides or photos.** Some photography stores will do this, or your video store may be able to refer you to an individual who specializes in custom-made videotapes from slides and prints.

Your Photos and Your Computer

Many film developers offer you the option of having your film digitized and put on a diskette. You can buy computer software that gives you a variety of innovative uses for photos that you can do at home. For example, you can e-mail them to friends, family and business associates, create your own computer photo album, produce your own slide show, or use your photos in letters.

Digital cameras are becoming very popular and affordable and a wonderful alternative to paper. Pictures are stored on your computer or CD-ROMs, and you print out only the ones you want. Furthermore you might find an online photoservice such as www.ofoto.com very useful. It allows you to create online photo albums, send pictures to friends and family, allows them to view photos, and best of all anyone you invite can order their own photos. Other options available include greeting cards and other photo products.

A friend of mine who recently had a baby finds this service optimal for keeping track of weekly milestones, sending pictures (often!) to grandparents out of town, yet reducing the paper in her life.

Keep Those Cards and Letters Coming

Okay, what do you do about all those beautiful greeting cards you've received for birthdays, anniversaries and other special events? What about all the letters from relatives and friends? If you keep them, you may feel guilty because they take up so much room, and if you toss them you may feel guilty because you care about the people who sent them or you think they're too pretty to throw away.

There is nothing wrong with keeping every card and letter you ever received if you have plenty of space to store them and you enjoy looking at them—or just entertain the possibility that you might someday. If, however, you feel a knot in your stomach every time you see them or you don't have a place to put the stationery you need for answering today's mail, then you would be wise to reconsider your actions.

One viable solution for letters is to select the ones that contain information that would be of particular interest to you in the future. I enjoy saving the letters from my mother that describe special family events, for example.

The method you use for keeping cards and letters will be determined by the way you plan to use them. If you are keeping them strictly for casual reading in the years to come, a box labeled Letters to Save will do nicely. If, however, you want to be able to refer to the letters, you should keep them accessible. Try filing them alphabetically in an accordion-type file with alphabet dividers.

I put all the cards I receive for a particular occasion on the mantle in the family room. After two or three weeks, I keep only those that are particularly special—and in some cases I throw them all away because I know there are others, and I am optimistic enough to believe there will be more! A friend of mine keeps all of hers and then every few years makes a collage of them to hang as a decoration. Another frames cards she finds particularly beautiful. Some community groups collect them to use in self-help projects for handicapped persons and senior citizens. Sometimes schools are happy to have them for art projects (see Recycling in Chapter 6).

Whatever you decide to do with them, remember that the sender intended that card or letter to bring joy, not stress—so enjoy!

The Kitchen Papers

The kitchen is the "heart" of many if not most homes. It's easy to see how it can also become a catchall for a multitude of paper—the newspaper that you left on the table when you hurried off to work or a morning school carpool; the school papers your kids brought home and dumped on the counter; the mail you grabbed out of the mailbox as you raced in the door (now sorted in several unidentified piles!); and the notes, phone messages and recipes that are piled on any available surface. How can you sort all this out?

Kitchen Catch-All

First, create a gathering place to put all the paper when you don't have time to put it away. You could use a large basket, a shelf or a tray. The key to successful kitchen-paper management is to make an appointment with yourself to get back to the pile before it becomes too overwhelming, to separate what should come out of the catch-all from what really belongs in the kitchen. You may find it helpful to do it on a regular basis—before your favorite television show, once a month when you pay bills—at a minimum when the container gets full.

Keep the catch-all pile as small as possible by putting things away whenever you can. For example, if as you pick up the mail you see several pieces of junk mail, throw them away immediately. It will also be much easier to keep the papers that need to remain in the kitchen at a minimum if you have specific places to put

> **Make sure the system you set up is easy for the person who is sorting the mail as well as the people who need to get the mail.**

other papers. Unread newspapers might go under the family-room coffee table; newspapers you've read could be placed on the floor in the front hall closet or in the garage to be saved for a community recycling program, or thrown out, and so on.

If your work center is in the kitchen, put the papers you need to act on in your To-Sort Tray until you are ready to take action. If your work center is in another room, take your papers there, whether it's an office, family room, bedroom or basement. Put the papers that belong to other family members in places designated for their attention. Make sure the system you set up is easy for the person who is sorting the mail as well as the people who need to get the mail.

Obviously some papers belong in the kitchen—recipes, cookbooks, entertainment records, coupons (but only if you are a user and not just a collector!), and take-out menus. We'll get to these papers soon.

Message Mania

One maddening result of our telephone-laden world is a myriad of notes—some written to us by others who have taken our telephone messages, some written by us to ourselves as we talk or plan to talk on the phone.

What can you do to avoid, or at least minimize, this problem? How many times a week do you find a piece of paper with notes from several different telephone conversations? The first question is, "Where do I put it?" A very simple solution is to get a small notepad by the phone—I like 5" x 7"—and use one piece of paper, more if necessary, for each call. When the conversation is over, ask yourself, "What is the next action required on this piece of paper?" The answer will tell you where to put it (see Chapter 11 for more details on this process). Often, all you need to do is double-check to see that the number is in your telephone-number system; then you can throw away one more piece of paper.

Designate a place where family members can check to see if they have phone messages. Use a bulletin board, a plastic message holder, magnets on the refrigerator or envelopes attached to the wall or a door. Be sure the owner's names are clearly labeled so there's no confusion. Encourage family members to note on the message the date and time they took the call.

Returning phone calls can be a big stumbling block. All the organization in the world won't make the phone-related papers go away. Only you, or someone to whom you delegate, can do that. See page 57 for some time-management tips that can help with regard to phone calls.

To keep your message center organized, find one place to put all the papers that require calls. Put them in an Action-File folder labeled Call, or in a pile near your phone. Or make a list of the people you need to call (and their phone numbers), and throw out the individual notes. Then when you have time to make one phone call it won't require much more time to make two or three.

FOR YOUR PHONE

Answering machines and services can do many things, including having multiple outgoing messages and separate "mail boxes" for each member of the household. Virtually all systems allow you to retrieve messages when you are away from home.

You can also use the memo capability so that if another family member wants to leave a message they can talk into the machine or the phone, and it will record their message as if it were a regular incoming message.

Designing Your Cookbook and Recipe System

Let's take a look at the issue of recipes and cookbooks. First of all, accept the fact that you may not organize your recipes and cookbooks the same way your mother did. That does not mean you are wrong—just different, because your lifestyle, priorities and needs are different from those of your mother. So erase from your mind those "shoulds" and think about what you need to make a system work for you.

If you think about it, you'll probably find that most of your cooking is done from less than 20% of your recipes. I've observed that the axiom "less is more" is especially true in the kitchen. The more recipes people have, the fewer they use. And we often spend more time

Don't wait to set up a system for today's recipes until you've conquered the backlog. It will be easier to set up a system for the recipes you are collecting now.

agonizing over the fact we don't use them—or chastising ourselves because we haven't organized them—than we do cooking them! The only solution is to put a stop to this negative cycle.

Don't wait to set up a system for today's recipes until you've conquered the backlog. It will be easier to set up a system for the recipes you are collecting now. Then incorporate the backlog into the new system as you have the time, energy and interest.

There are dozens of systems on the market for organizing recipes. If you've found one that suits your needs, by all means use it, but I've found that many of them do not allow for the flexibility that is essential to create a system that is workable for particular situations. For example, the categories may not be the same as you would use, or the space allowed to write, type, or glue the recipe isn't large enough.

This is not a place to let your perfectionism get in the way of starting the task. The system doesn't need to be perfect, and probably won't be. You can always make adjustments as you experiment.

One of the easiest ways to get started is with file folders so you can sort your recipes into categories. Designate a place, preferably in or near the kitchen, where you will keep recipes. Put all the supplies you will need there: file folders, felt-tip pen to label the files, scissors, tape, index cards, recipe cards, blank recipe book or whatever system you plan to use.

Your Recipe Categories

There are dozens of ways to categorize recipes—just compare cookbook indexes, if you doubt it—so don't worry about what categories you want to use. Instead of trying to think up the categories first, start with the recipes you have. Ask yourself, "If I were looking for this recipe, what would I think of?"

As a rule, start with broader categories first, such as Bread. Then if the quantity of recipes in that category becomes too bulky to manage, you can subdivide the category into Yeast Breads, Muffins, Sweet Breads, etc. If you spend a great deal of time cooking and entertaining and enjoy taking the time to plan menus, test new recipes, etc., then you may want your categories to be very specific from the start.

I find it helpful to separate the tried-and-true recipes from those I would like to try, which remain in the file folders. When I'm convinced a recipe is a winner—and I don't keep it unless it is—I put it on a 4" x 6" index card and into a card box. It is not necessary to type or handwrite the recipe unless you particularly want to. The fastest way is to cut and paste the recipe to fit on the index card. (You may wish to make notes on the card about when you served it, to whom, what you served with it, or suggestions for adaptations of the recipe.) The box is divided into categories the same way I divided the recipes in the manila file folders. A loose-leaf notebook will also work well.

Decide whether to separate your microwave recipes from your conventional recipes. Many conventional recipes can be adapted to microwave, but many people think of them quite separately.

The Recipe Search
If you are frequently frustrated because you can't find a recipe from one of your many cookbooks that you used successfully on a previous occasion, put a note that includes the recipe title, cookbook and page number in the appropriate category in your recipe file.

Another option is to create a separate notebook divided into the same categories you use for organizing your recipes. Whenever you find a recipe you like in a cookbook, enter the name of the recipe with the title of the cookbook and page number where you found the recipe.

Conquering the Recipe Backlog
Once you have a recipe system set up and working, you can decide whether you want to tackle the backlog. You may decide it makes more sense to toss the entire collection.

If you want to incorporate your existing recipes, set aside enough time to do it. How much time you'll need

> **When I'm convinced a recipe is a winner—and I don't keep it unless it is—I put it on a 4" x 6" index card and into a card box.**

KITCHEN TRANSITIONS

Your attitude toward the kitchen, and toward cooking, will determine to a great extent how your kitchen should be organized. There are many factors that contribute to our feelings, and it is important to acknowledge that these feelings change with time and circumstances. This doesn't mean we're lazy or negligent, just that our priorities have changed.

I have clients who are overwhelmed with guilt by the piles of kitchen papers because they're afraid to admit that they aren't as interested in cooking as they once were. In fact, I'm a good example. When I was first married, my husband and I entertained often. We had three children and we were on a limited budget. Therefore, I spent a considerable amount of time with papers in the kitchen—collecting coupons, selecting recipes, keeping records of what I served guests, educating myself about the nutritional needs of my children, and reading the food columns in the newspapers.

Later, I was divorced and my children were with me only part time. I ate out often and devoted the energy previously spent in the kitchen on my career. Then I married a man who has two children.

With five teenagers in and out of our home, the organization needs in the kitchen changed drastically. Because family members—and their friends—are in and out frequently, it's important to have lots of food possibilities at a moment's notice.

Once again I became interested in recipes, but very different ones from those that interested me 15 years before. For example, I used to believe that if I didn't spend at least an hour preparing the evening meal, no compliment was justified. Now I was looking for 10-minute recipes that would generate smiles—or at least fill stomachs! In addition, much of my cooking now is done in the microwave. And I'm much more conscious of the nutritional value of what we eat. Entertaining is much more informal, so soufflés that have to be eaten the moment they come out of the oven are of little interest. Dishes that can be prepared in advance of the event are essential.

Once I understood that my circumstances had changed, I went through all my old recipes, and the recipes I intended to try. If a recipe didn't fit my time requirements or the dish wouldn't be healthy, I threw the recipe out—at least most of them!

Now my children are grown and out of our home. My husband and I eat out frequently, but we entertain often, so once again my patterns are changing.

depends on how much you have, what you think about the project, your working style and circumstances. Will you enjoy the project and want to spend a long time on it? Or will you regard it as a frustrating one for which you will have a limited attention span? Do circumstances dictate that it will be done on a piecemeal basis, even though you would prefer to spend more time at it? Once you have made the decision to organize the backlog, formalize your commitment by making an appointment with yourself and setting aside the time on your calendar.

Is there a family member or friend who will help you? If so, get them involved in the appointment so you'll be less likely to ignore it. If organizing the recipes is a major problem for you, hire a professional organizer—"Yes, Virginia, there are people who are good enough, and like it enough, to get paid for organizing recipes."

After you've decided when you're going to conquer the backlog, determine where you will do it. If at all possible, find a spot you can use until the project is completed. (I declared the dining room off limits to the family for two weeks and did it there.) Or set up a card table in the corner of a room. It will be much easier, and less frustrating, if you don't have to get everything out each time you want to work—and you may find that you will work a few minutes here and there, unplanned, if everything is accessible. With a cordless phone you can talk to a friend and organize recipes at the same time.

The next step is to collect all the recipes you have—or just some of them to start if looking at them all is too overwhelming—and get organized. Undoubtedly along the way you will get discouraged and overwhelmed. Keep asking yourself: "Do I really need this recipe? Does it exist somewhere else? How long has it been since I've used, or had, the recipe? What's the worst possible thing that would happen if I tossed it?" As you sort, you may well discover that your standards change as you realize how much work is involved to keep everything you had planned to keep.

Trying New Recipes

One of the essential steps in keeping the recipes under control is developing a method for trying new ones. Whenever I feel like I'm in a cooking rut or if I have

> **One of the essential steps in keeping the recipes under control is developing a method for trying new ones.**

A FAMILY TELEPHONE LOG

A telephone log—usually used in offices—can be adapted for home use. Try using a simple spiral notebook, which stays open to the last entry. Whenever someone takes a message they enter it in the book. To the left of the message, put the name of the person the message is for. (I like the 6" x 9" size—there's enough space to write, but it doesn't take up too much space on the counter.)

some extra time, I choose six to eight recipes I would like to try in the next few weeks. Usually I pick one or two main dishes, one or two salads or vegetables, one or two soups, and one or two desserts.

When you've selected the recipes you want to try, take time to note on your shopping list the ingredients you will need to prepare these dishes. (Obviously, any perishable items can't be purchased too far in advance.) Then clip the recipes to a magnet on the refrigerator or put them in a special compartment in your recipe box or book. When you are rushed to get dinner on the table but want to try something new you will have the menu idea and the ingredients right at your finger tips. (The same technique can be used in choosing recipes that your children can prepare if they cook while you are working.)

The final step in this system is making a decision about the recipe after you have eaten the results. Was it great? If not, why keep it? Avoid the "I really should give it one more try" syndrome. There are thousands more recipes you can try that might be great, so let it go! Then your recipe collection becomes something you really treasure instead of tolerate.

One winter I was snowbound for four days. I had a wonderful time experimenting with my new recipes. In addition, I ended up with a freezer full of food that could be microwaved for a speedy nutritious meal on the days following the snow when I was too busy catching up on lost time to spend time cooking.

Entertainment Records

One of my clients had invited a certain gentleman to her home on several occasions with various dinner guests. She was most embarrassed to discover that she had served tomatoes stuffed with spinach on the last three occasions. (Unfortunately, he didn't like it the first time!)

One way to avoid that problem is to create a notebook to record your entertaining. Just as with the recipes, there are various ways to organize this notebook. If you entertain lavishly and frequently have the same guests, it will require more time to maintain the system than if you entertain simply and/or infrequently. The simplest way is to list the events in chronological order. Include the menu, table decorations, guest list (and seating arrangement, if you wish), and perhaps even what you wore. Consider recording your thoughts about improvements you want to make when you entertain again. That could be making a slight change in a recipe (and note the change on your recipe card or in your recipe book), a possible change in serving logistics (serve the coffee on a separate table, or put out small forks with the appetizers), or a note about the flowers.

If you entertain frequently and are particularly concerned about not duplicating menus for the same guests, you could put a separate alphabetical section in your book. Each guest would have a small section where you could put the date when you entertained him or her. Then you could check the chronological list for the menu that guest was served. For example, under "A", you would have: Adams, John—3/6/01; 10/2/01; 5/4/02; etc. You could also note there any items of concern when entertaining that guest—allergies, food preferences, medical concerns, etc.

To Market, To Market

It's tough to keep track of the food we have on hand and the food we need to purchase There are paper-management techniques you can use to simplify your shopping trips. If you do the majority of your shopping in the same store, create a checklist of the items you most frequently purchase, arranged in the order of the grocery store aisles. Leave space in each section for special items that are not regularly on the list.

Make a dozen copies. After you've tried the system that many times, you will probably find ways you want to change the form. I find it helpful to have the shopping list posted on the refrigerator, with a pencil permanently attached with a string. Then I or another member of the family can check off items as we see we need them. However, if there are family members who are unable or unwilling to use the list, it might be easier to transfer the ad hoc list from the refrigerator onto the form just before you go to the store.

If you have problems with people forgetting to put items on the list when they use the last of something, try making a list of commonly used items, or if you type the list on your computer, type these items in bold face. Then, just before you do a major shopping, you can make a quick check to see which of those items are low in supply.

PUT IT ON THE FRIDGE

Communication can be a constant frustration in families, particularly in homes where there is a single parent or where both parents are working. To improve the situation, designate a communication center that is convenient for everyone. The refrigerator is usually a good place to put chore reminders. But be sure your messages aren't always things to do. You can also communicate nonessential, but very important messages, such as "Hope you had a good day at school. I love you, Mom."

Coupon Coordination

A discussion of kitchen papers wouldn't be complete without including coupons. Decision-making and organization—in that order—are the keys to saving money with manufacturers coupons and refund offers.

The first decision to make is whether you are really committed to the idea of coupon clipping. My opinion is that unless you enjoy doing it or your budget requires it, coupon saving is too much trouble. Ask yourself, "Do I really save money when I consider the time it takes me? Do I end up buying more expensive products that I wouldn't necessarily buy if I didn't have the coupon? Is clipping coupons an attempt to assuage my guilty feelings over excess spending habits, or an effort to appease my mother?" One man I know looks at coupon clipping as a game and uses it for relaxation.

Many people clip coupons only for those products they routinely buy, such as coffee, laundry soap and paper products. Other people spend two to three hours a week clipping and can save $30 to $50 per week on grocery purchases, in addition to the amount received in cash from rebate offers. I read in a newspaper about one woman who bought $113.05 worth of groceries for $1.69. The real price: Her office is a corner of the basement, where she has organized coupons, labels and proofs of purchases into 14 grocery bags, six cardboard boxes, eight filing-cabinet drawers and a bookcase! "This kind of couponing is available to anyone who is willing to get organized," she said, peering over the mountain of groceries in her cart.

The basic principle of organizing, put like things together, certainly applies to coupons. Establish categories for your coupons in the same way you establish categories for your recipes. Ask yourself, "What category would I think of if I wanted this coupon?"

There are several possibilities for categories, such as Paper Products, Cleaning Products, and Vegetables (this category could be broken down in Vegetables—Frozen, and Vegetables—Canned). You may want a separate system for refunds, which could be located in the same container, but in a separate section. Within that system, you would have the same categories as you had for coupons. In addition, you might want a section for Refunds in Progress.

Keep a supply of return-address labels, envelopes and stamps on hand. For a refund offer that requires several proof-of-purchase labels, put the labels in a pre-addressed envelope that has the refund expiration date on the top right-hand corner where it can be covered by the stamp before you mail the refund.

The technique you use for storing coupons is also important. Decide whether you will always carry all your coupons with you when you go to the store or whether you will have a Master Coupon Box at home from which

Establish categories for your coupons in the same way you establish categories for your recipes.

you can pull out those coupons you want to take with you. While at the store, you can use a regular business-size envelope (or several) or you can purchase a coupon billfold designed specifically for that purpose. It is unlikely that the categories in a pre-designed system will be the same as yours, so feel free to put on your own labels to make the system work for you. However you choose to keep the coupons, be sure to purge expired ones on a regular basis.

A woman I know divides her coupons according to the shopping aisles in her local store. Not only does the system add continuity to her coupon and refund hobby, but it saves her an incredible amount of time.

There is no right or wrong decision on this issue. Experiment until you find a method that works. Just decide, recognizing that you can change your decision at any time based on your current circumstances. Once your decision is made, concentrate on setting up the system needed to make the decision workable. But above all, create a system that gives you a feeling of success.

Children and Paper

Children and paper go hand-in-hand in our society. As soon as a couple even begins to think about starting a family, the paper begins to accumulate—information on childbirth classes, ads from child-care services, notices of mother's-day-out programs, descriptions of child-rearing techniques, articles on overcoming fertility problems, and books about the psychological impact of parenting and the how-to's of surviving parenthood.

There are numerous approaches to surviving this paper blizzard, but the first and most important step (as with any paper-management issue) is to start some kind of system. As your children grow older, the system will need to change, but you don't need to worry about that now.

For the Parent-to-Be

The first step toward establishing a system that will work for you is to examine your own feelings about keeping and using information. Is it important to you to have easy access to articles about child rearing or would you be more likely to ask your doctor, a psychologist or discuss it with your parents or a friend? Do you need the information near you to feel secure, even if you never use it? Or does having paper around create additional stress, guilt or frustration? Is it realistic that you will take the time and effort required to maintain an extensive library or is there someone else in the family who will help you? These are important questions to answer to prevent setting unrealistic standards for yourself. You create a no-win situation if you feel guilty because you keep too much, and feel guilty if you don't. Eliminate the "shoulds," and acknowledge what will work for you.

Collect and Categorize

The simplest way to begin any system is to collect all the information you have into the largest general category. In this case, that's Children. Find a container, a basket, shelf or file folder and label it clearly.

When there is more information than can be easily handled and the file folder becomes too bulky, divide the information into the next logical categories. For example, information about children can be categorized into areas of concern, such as education, medical, memorabilia, legal information, and toys and equipment. Notice that toys and equipment are put together; it is often too difficult to differentiate between the categories. However, you may have Toys and Equipment—Owned and Toys and Equipment—Shopping Information.

Our needs are constantly changing. A system that works when a child is six months old might be totally inappropriate when she is sixteen, and the system that works when she is sixteen will be overkill when she is twenty.

For example, when your child is in elementary school, a Reference File labeled Susan—Education may be sufficient. However, when she enters high school that category may be too general. The categories you will need at this point depend on your particular style and on your child's interests. If you are very active in your educational program, you may need a file for PTA, College Preparation, or Extracurricular Activities. (That last category might need to be subdivided into Gymnastics, Scouts, etc.) And when your child has gone off to college, many of these Reference Files will no longer be necessary. At this point all the report cards for kindergarten through high school become highly irrelevant. Choose one or two for your grandchildren to see. If you want to keep all the files about your child together, put the child's name at the beginning of each label: Susan—Education and Susan—Sports, for example.

GRANDPARENTING AND PAPER

Having recently become a grandmother, I can't resist the temptation to mention how important managing paper can be in this role! I've had great fun with my children working out ways to cope with all the new paper in their lives, as well as creating new files of my own with resources for becoming Grandparent of the Century!

If you know that you will not take the time to develop a detailed filing system, find a basket, shelf or file folder and label it John—Education. It may take you 10 minutes to go through the entire box if you need a copy of an award certificate to go with a college application, but it will be a massive improvement over having all the members of the family turning the house upside down looking for that large brown envelope!

Teach Your Children Well

With all the obligations and options in today's world, it is very easy for a parent to spend an inordinate amount of time being a social secretary, or just a nagger. Teaching your child organizational skills will benefit you and your child—for life!

One of the biggest problems we all face is making choices. Over and over I find houses buried in paper because adults feel compelled to do it all—read every book, newspaper and magazine, keep every photo and memento, or go to every concert, seminar and reception. Living a happy and healthy life, or even just getting by, in today's world means making choices. Remember, clutter is postponed decisions. As parents we should teach that concept to our children, and one place to begin is with paper.

There are many steps you can take to help your children learn how to manage the paper in their lives, as well as to become good time managers.

As soon as your child goes into an organized play-

CREATIVE USES FOR ARTWORK

Put several creations together and make a collage for your child's wall or to use as a present for a relative. Grandparents, aunts and uncles are delighted to receive letters from children. Have your child write a short message on the back of the painting, or just send the painting—signed, of course! Teach your child the value of recycling. Artwork makes wonderful wrapping paper for gifts—especially for admiring grandparents!

group or educational program, you will begin to accumulate paper. Designate a special place for her to put the papers she brings home from school. If you start this habit early, you will avoid many panic situations of trying to find a trip permission slip when you should be getting ready for work or running out the door to catch the car pool. Each evening or first thing in the morning you can check and see what came home from school and what requires your attention.

The Art Gallery

It's always a challenge to cope with your child's creative work. Young children can produce enough paper to fill a small art gallery within a week. Which of those 400 finger-painted gems will become cherished examples of the early works of future Picassos?

There's nothing wrong with keeping everything that children create if we have plenty of space to keep it, and plenty of energy to organize it. But few people have either. It's easy to get caught in the trap of feeling guilty if we throw away the things our children make, and feeling overwhelmed if we don't. It is essential to involve your children in the selection process from the beginning.

You can use this process as a tool for teaching them decision-making techniques, which will be important for them to know as they grow up. In my experience, one of the major contributors to the problems that adults have

YOU'LL SEE RESULTS LATER

Caveat: Just because you teach your children how to organize doesn't mean you'll see the results. However, it has been my experience that as they get older and see the benefits to organization, they will begin to practice what you've taught them.

with organization of their papers—and often their lives—is their mistaken notion that in order to be organized, they must have everything and do everything. Not true!

All the papers you'd like to keep can be put in a basket, or on a bulletin board with your child's name prominently displayed. Then when the basket gets full or the bulletin board gets crowded, encourage your child to choose her three favorite papers, which can be put in a Memorabilia Box for safekeeping. Put the child's name, age, and date on the back of the artwork to make it more meaningful 20 years from now.

Kids and Calendars

Once your children reach a certain age there are many other steps you can take to help them learn how to manage their paper and to improve their time-management skills. For example, put a large calendar with plenty of writing space in an easily accessible place. The refrigerator is a good choice, because everyone ends up there sooner or later.

Have each child note when he or she needs transportation to soccer, cookies for a school party, or plans to spend the night at a friend's house. This method helps you plan your schedule and avoids last-minute crises— and can teach your child a lesson in responsibility. If your son comes running to you at the last minute and says, "Mom, I need a ride to gymnastics," you can say, "I didn't see it on the calendar, son, and I can't take you right now." If he misses an important practice or is late for his game, it won't take him long to realize that he has

A COLORFUL CALENDAR

Consider using different colored pens for each member of the family, and attach the pens with a long string next to the calendar on your refrigerator so you won't hear the excuse "I couldn't find a pencil!"

to take some responsibility for his own life. Of course, you have to take into account unusual circumstances and make exceptions when you feel it is appropriate to do so.

Don't forget that you owe the same courtesy to your children. For the career parent, this is a great place to communicate facts about your schedule that will affect your son or daughter. Include travel schedules, night meetings or houseguests.

As soon as your child begins getting school assignments in advance, help him choose an assignment book. Teach him how to plot out complicated assignments by reading one-half chapter each day—or if it works better to read two chapters at a time, choose those days on which there are not other obligations, such as piano lessons or soccer practice. Discuss the concept of choosing styles. Remind him to watch for family commitments that might affect his schedule. Recognize that his style may not be the same as yours, but that doesn't mean it's wrong.

Encourage your children to use a calendar to keep track of sports events, babysitting commitments, job responsibilities at home, birthdays they want to remember, etc.

The calendar is also an excellent place to help your child understand the importance of goal setting. If, for example, your daughter really wants to take a trip this summer that you feel is too expensive, or you feel she should contribute to the cost, help her plan how she could make it happen by using the calendar. Count the number of weeks until she needs the money and determine how much she will have to make every week if she is to succeed. She can use the calendar to block out time when she will work and set goals for raising the money.

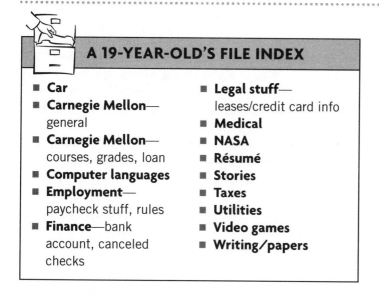

A 19-YEAR-OLD'S FILE INDEX

- **Car**
- **Carnegie Mellon**—general
- **Carnegie Mellon**—courses, grades, loan
- **Computer languages**
- **Employment**—paycheck stuff, rules
- **Finance**—bank account, canceled checks

- **Legal stuff**—leases/credit card info
- **Medical**
- **NASA**
- **Résumé**
- **Stories**
- **Taxes**
- **Utilities**
- **Video games**
- **Writing/papers**

Your Child's Own Files

As your child gets older, help him organize the papers he needs to cope with daily life. Purchase several file folders and help label them according to his needs. Make a category for each subject at school and each area of interest. At the end of the year encourage your child (and assist if necessary) to clean out the files and determine what papers he would like to keep as mementos, and which have served their purpose and can be thrown away.

If your children are involved in several organizations, a Reference File called Directories can be very useful to keep the lists of participant's names that you receive from scouts, sports, school, youth group, etc. This file can save many hassles when Saturday morning rolls around and you are madly trying to find a ride to soccer for your child. The information is also helpful if your child is sending out party invitations or trying to locate a friend's phone number or address.

My 15-year-old son stopped in my office one day and noticed on my desk an X-Rack—a plastic frame designed to hold hanging file folders. He's a gadget lover and interested in art. He asked if I would get him one. The combination of the uniqueness of the file holder and the bright-colored file folders with plastic tabs fascinated him—and gave me a terrific opening to help him in setting up a file system for his needs. It is very important to do whatever you can to make the organizing process appeal to your child. It's a great way to create one-on-one time, and you benefit doubly because both you and your child's lives will run more smoothly.

Your child may also want files that relate to special interests. For example, your teenager might want a category on Fashion or Shopping Ideas to take on her next shopping trip.

Be sure your child makes a File Index or list of the files to keep in the very front of the files. For an example of one 19-year-old's file categories, see the box on page 161.

CHAPTER 21

Travel and Papers

Travel is a good example of how paperwork has multiplied in today's world: bonus programs for airline travel, car rentals and hotel accommodations. Entire books have been written, newsletters published and computer software designed to make it easier for the traveler to take advantage of all the offers. Not taking advantage of such offers creates the same kind of emotion in us as not submitting our medical expenses to the insurance company for reimbursement.

All That Paraphernalia

Travel brings with it other kinds of paper problems as well: maps, directions, confirmations, tickets, itineraries, notes about people to see and things to do, papers we need to take with us on the trip, addresses and phone numbers, traveler's checks, passports and all the identification cards with numbers you need to get credit for those fabulous bonus programs.

Then there are all the papers you collect while you are traveling: more maps, phone numbers and addresses of new friends made, favorite restaurants and shops, receipts for purchases that are being shipped to you, boarding passes and ticket stubs, travel brochures and a variety of memorabilia.

If your trip involved any meetings, you'll undoubtedly have a pile of papers that contain all kinds of wonderful information you want to keep or use.

You arrive home from the trip with the best of intentions about going through all those papers, but as soon as you walk in the door you're confronted with all the mail that arrived while you were away. So it is likely that the trip papers are pushed aside so you can deal with more-pressing matters. After several weeks, you get tired of looking at them or you have company coming and need to clear off the table, so into a drawer they go, never to be seen again!

Do you cut out travel articles? Collect travel magazines or reviews about travel books? In order for them to be useful to you, you need to organize them. When was the last time you went through a pile of old magazines to find that article about the terrific restaurant in San Francisco?

Let's take a look at the various areas and see what can be done to manage the travel-related paper in our lives.

Essential Information

First of all, consider the travel information you want to keep for reference. This would include maps, travel brochures, information from past trips, newsletters from travel services and bonus-program information. The first step is to get all the information together. If you have a small amount, you may need something as simple as a file folder or a box labeled Travel Information. But if you have more than will fit into one category comfortably you need to decide how to organize the information. One way would be to group it by category. Make a pile for maps, another for airline information, another for travel brochures, etc. These could then be incorporated into your Reference File under Travel, so the labels would look like this: Travel—Airline Information, Travel—Brochures, Travel—Receipts, etc.

You might also find it helpful to put frequent-flier information on your rotary card file, along with the phone numbers of the airlines.

If you participate in several frequent flyer programs, you'll need a separate Reference File for each airline, so you would have a series of files such as Airlines—American, Airlines—United, Airlines—Delta, etc. If you're horrified at the thought of so many files, consider this:

FOR THE FREQUENT TRAVELER

Consider creating a wallet-size card with all your airline, hotel and car-rental numbers. It's a great space saver— and it's fun to see the reaction of the desk agent!

You're rushing out the door to grab a flight. The last thing you need to do is go through a pile of papers from an airline you're not taking. It will take only a second to grab the information from the appropriate airline file. As an alternative, bookmark Web sites and register for frequent-flier information electronically.

You will discover that your airline files become bulky very quickly, so it is important to establish your retention guidelines. I would suggest you keep your monthly mileage statements for as long as you participate in the program because airlines sometimes offer special bonuses to travelers who have accumulated a certain number of miles during a certain period of time. Most airlines send a monthly newsletter. Keep only the latest one, unless there is specific information in an older newsletter. If so, mark clearly what information interests you so that you quickly identify why you kept that particular newsletter.

This same system will work for hotel and car-rental bonus programs. Of course, the most important information to have is your membership number.

One of the other complicating factors in this issue are the tie-in programs. For example, certain airlines have reciprocal privileges. Or, if you fly one airline and rent your car from a tie-in agency, you can get bonus miles. There are several books and newsletters on the market that describe these offers. If you're serious about collecting bonus points, one of them might be worth your investment.

Maps and Brochures

Maps can be another paper problem for the traveler. If you have only a dozen maps or so, one Reference File or a box will be plenty, but if you have more than that, re-

MAKE A PRE-TRIP CHECKLIST

This can help you remember those last-minute tasks that are easy to forget, such as "check thermostat," "turn off coffeepot," "stop newspaper," and "arrange for plant and pet care."

fine your system by geographic area. I started with U.S.—Northeast, U.S.—Northwest, U.S.—Southeast, U.S.—Southwest. As my travel increased dramatically, I now have one file for every state and several for foreign countries.

What about travel brochures? To determine how these should be filed, you need to identify why you are keeping them at all. The answer might not be the same for each brochure. You might be keeping one strictly as a memento of a beautiful experience, another as a reference in case you return, or another to share with a friend. Ask yourself, "Under what circumstances would I want this information?" The answer will help you determine where you should file it. Put a date on the brochure when you file it so it will be easier to clean out the files in the years to come.

If you have more than eight to ten travel files, I suggest you create a separate filing system—say, a separate drawer—for travel, rather than incorporating them into your existing Reference Files. Identify travel files with a particular color so you can recognize them easily.

Before the Trip

As soon as you begin planning for any trip, make an Action File with the destination on the label, such as New York. This will provide an immediate place to put any information regarding the trip—tickets, itinerary, reminders of things you want to take with you, contacts you want to make while you are there, or places you want to visit or shop. You may have several trip files at one time.

If you travel frequently, make a standard packing

list. Keep it in your to-do book or in your suitcase. Then as soon as you begin planning a trip, take the list and put it in the destination file. As you think of things you want to take with you, note them on the packing list.

When you pack your suitcase, check off each item and note the specific number taken. For example, Dress Shirts—6. (One client puts her list in a plastic folder and uses a grease pencil to check it off. Then it can be easily erased after each use.) If you are concerned about losing your luggage and being able to substantiate a claim, keep the list until you return from the trip.

People who travel with children can use the list to help their children get everything repacked in the suitcase. When my daughter was twelve, she decided to take the list with her so that when she was repacking her suitcase, she could check it off to be sure she remembered to bring everything home with her.

If you've filed your travel reference material by geographical area, it will be very easy to check that file for any additional information you might want on a particular trip. Sometimes I even take the file with me for airplane reading. Be sure to take a list of frequent-flier numbers. These could be listed in your to-do book under Travel or Numbers.

> ### FAMILY FUN
>
> If you or your family enjoy taking day trips but have difficulty thinking where to go on the spur of the moment, create a Day Trip Ideas Reference File. Information in the file can also help when you have house guests. Vacation Ideas can also be a useful file when it is time to decide on a summer vacation plan.

On the Trip

If you are going to attend any kind of meeting while you're on the trip and will be collecting a number of papers, I suggest you create Action Files for the trip. It will be easier to make decisions about what you want to do with the papers as you acquire them than it will be to go back through the papers when you return home. These files might include Write, File, Pending (see Chapter 11).

What about travel receipts? You can't decide what to do with a receipt unless you know why it is useful to you. Do you need it to prove a tax deductible expense? If so, it could go with other tax information for the year (see Chapter 14). Are you keeping it until the china that you purchased arrives safely? If so, it could go in a Pending Action File (see Chapter 11). When the china arrives, the receipt could go in a Personal-Property Reference File in case you need it to substantiate an insurance claim.

After the Trip

When the trip is over, put your ticket stub and boarding passes in the airline file until you are certain your miles have been credited to your account. Then throw the boarding passes away. File the ticket stub only if you need it for a specific reason—for example, a business reimbursement or a tax-deductible expense. Otherwise, throw it away.

Take action on any papers you have brought home with you or incorporate them into your existing Action Files.

Finally, be sure to purge the trip Action File itself. Throw away any information that is no longer relevant and file the remaining information into the appropriate Reference File.

Suppose, for example, you meet someone on a trip who lives in another city you visit frequently, or hope to visit one day. Put her name and address with a note about where you met in that geographical file. Does all this sound like too much drudgery? It may be a lifesaver if you find yourself stranded in her city one day, or just a lot of fun if you get together and reminisce about all the fun you had on that Caribbean cruise.

Home Computers and Paper

There are many books on the subject of personal computers. This is not the place for a major discussion about them, but it would be foolish to write a book about paper management in this day and age without mentioning personal computers. They can, without a doubt, do many miraculous things to help us manage our lives more effectively. They will not, however, solve a paper-management problem.

In fact, if a personal computer is used improperly it can complicate paper management considerably because it's so easy to create more paper. For example, you write a letter or a report and print out a copy to edit it. When you have completed the editing and entered the changes in the computer, you print out another copy. Within minutes you have doubled the amount of paper in your life.

Too Many Printouts

The computer will not make decisions for you. For example, people who have computers with programs that print special reports, especially home account systems, often feel compelled to print out every report possible to ensure that they are getting the most out of their computer. What they often get is confused.

This is also a major reason that paper gets out of hand. The best approach is to print one of each report the first time or two you use a new program. Then study the reports and determine which ones are useful to you, and print only those. Keep in mind that any paper is of extremely limited value to you if you cannot identify specifically why you are keeping it. Ask yourself that (by now familiar) question, "Under what circumstances would I use this information?" This not only cuts down on the amount of paper, it also cuts down on the amount of confusion.

Store printed computer reports in your filing system whenever possible. For reports too large for the system, use binders to make the papers easier to manage and refer to. Label the binder as to contents and date. This will speed up the purging process considerably and make the binders easier to access while they are still useful.

Make Your Computer Work for You

A computer can simplify many of your paper-management tasks. The computer is an excellent tool for maintaining a File Index. However, you will find it helpful to print out two copies—one to keep in front of your Reference Files and another at your desk. If you travel frequently and collect papers as you go, carrying your File Index—so you can put the key filing word on papers as you get them—will go a long way toward eliminating a paper pile-up. Make entries and deletions by hand, and then periodically update it on the computer.

Kiplinger's *Taming the Paper Tiger* software program's sort capabilities eliminate the problem of deciding what to call a file because you assign files random numbers instead of titles and keep descriptions in the computer, which can find anything in seconds.

There are other programs designed to replace or supplement your calendar and your to-do list. These programs are becoming more popular with the advent of more portable notebook computers.

One of the most common uses of a computer in the home is for financial management. The biggest advantage of a computer over a manual system is that you will be forced to be consistent. It takes time to learn how to use the system, but many people have found it made a miraculous difference in their ability to manage their money.

PREVENTING DISASTER

The only thing between a computer and a computer crash is time. There are several ways you can back-up your computer data. Copying your data onto floppy disks works, but can be very time consuming if you have lots of files. (Have two sets of back-up disks, and alternate using them.) You can also install a tape back-up system into your computer.

If you have lots of data, a high-capacity removable tape back-up unit and good back-up software are helpful. A removable system can automatically and easily do a daily back-up. You can tell the computer to do a modified backup—only those documents that have changed since the last time you backed up. An online back-up service is another option.

The most important thing is that, whatever way you choose, you do it consistently. How often will depend on how much you value your time and how critical the work is that you are doing.

Another important disaster-prevention measure is virus protection. If you use e-mail, it is essential and will prevent lots of embarrassment by eliminating—or at least minimizing—the possibility of spreading a virus.

Even if you decide not to use a complete money-management package, you can use your word-processing program for keeping track of numerous records. For example, if you are frustrated keeping track of membership and subscription records, you can list all of them in alphabetical order, with the date you renewed and for how long. The next time you get a bill for a magazine, pull up your list on the screen and you will know how long before the subscription actually expires. The same system works well for keeping track of charitable donations.

You can even organize your recipes. But before you take that step, be sure the results will be worth the time and energy it will take to enter the data and to maintain it.

Computer Copy Versus Hard Copy

Many people believe that it must be preferable to keep documents in their computer rather than in their filing system. But consider this: If I have 100 documents in hard copy and you have the same 100 documents in the computer—or on floppy disks—which of us will find a particular document more quickly? In most cases, I will. It takes time to scroll down your computer screen to bring up each one of those documents.

My recommendation is to use your computer to store documents that you will be updating or using again. However, for one-time documents, such as a thank you letter or a memo, keep a copy in your Reference Files and then only if you might want to refer to it.

Organizing Your Computer Documents

Have you ever sat in front of your computer scrolling up and down the screen looking for a particular document you entered a few months ago, last week— or even yesterday? And heaven forbid if someone else entered it and you are trying to find it!

The easiest way to organize your files, and to back-up your computer, is to put all your data into one folder. Microsoft has created one called My Documents. You can create a subfolder for each program that you use, such as *Word, Excel, TaxCut, Paper Tiger, Power Point,* etc. Then, for example, when you create a *Word* document, you go to Save As, then to My Documents/Word, and name the document with words and phrases up to 255 characters. (Example, My Documents/Word/ Mary Stowe letter, PTA program suggestion, ethics, May 2002.) By naming a file or document with multiple keywords and phrases you can use the Find feature on the Start Menu to search on any of the words.

Computers for Communication, Fun and Education

The opportunities for using a computer at home are endless. On the communication side, you can use a variety of fonts and graphics to create your own letter-

> ## COMPUTER CLEAN-UP
>
> One of the major causes of computer problems is lack of memory, which can often be cured by cleaning out unnecessary files. To maximize your computer's performance, go to Start, Programs, Accessories, and use the available System Tools. Keep in mind that when you open your e-mail program, all the messages are loaded, so be sure to practice The Art of Wastebasketry with your e-mail frequently—and empty the e-mail trash!

head for personal and business correspondence, as well as write the letter. You can print invitations and flyers, or even publish a family newsletter.

Perhaps the most valuable application of the computer at home is for managing your financial life—paying bills, figuring taxes, and keeping track of insurance claims. It is also an excellent place to keep track of the important records we discussed in Chapter 17.

In my experience, one of the most rewarding uses of the computer has been to keep track of donations, memberships and magazine subscriptions. I create one document for each subject. I list the name of the subscription or organization with the date of payment and the expiration date. When I get a renewal notice or request for a donation, it's easy to obtain the information I need to make the decision.

The Internet offers unlimited opportunities for gathering all kinds of valuable information—materials for researching school reports, consumer issues, genealogy, travel or finances, just to name a few. Of course, you also have the option to print out this material, which makes your filing system even more crucial.

With all these opportunities comes another challenge: organizing and maintaining your computer. If you choose to file the information in your computer, create a consistent way of naming documents so that you will be able to retrieve them again. And above all, if losing the information in your computer would be a problem, establish a reliable way and a consistent schedule to back it up.

Children and Computers

Kids and computers go together. In fact, in many ways, they lead the way for fearful adults. Establish guidelines for your children's use of computers. If your children use your word-processing program, create a separate directory in the computer for each child. If they create materials they want to retrieve again, teach them to use subdirectories to organize their documents, or use the keyword method described above.

More Recycling Opportunities

There are several things you can do with your used computer paper instead of simply tossing it. Use the backside for drafts. Or cut the paper into various sizes to use as scratch paper beside your telephones and in the kitchen. If you prefer pads, you can take the paper to a commercial printer and have it cut and padded into handy pads for a small charge. (And, of course, there's always the bottom of the bird cage!)

You can even recycle your computer. Use your Zip code to find local recycling options for computers and other materials. Check out www.1800cleanup.org. For information on passing your computer along to a charity or school, go to http://sharetechnology.org.

"Paperholics"

For most of us, paper management is something we can live with. For others it is an insurmountable struggle. Their daily lives are seriously hampered, and in some cases brought to a standstill, by the endless clutter of unfinished projects, unread newspapers, magazines and books, unanswered mail and unfiled paper in unidentified piles, bags, and boxes throughout the house. I call these people "paperholics."

Each individual may feel unique, but thousands of people experience the same distress. For some, this constant stress can lead to physical ailments. Some paperholics live in fear of being discovered and go to great lengths to avoid having people come to their homes. Some even close off parts of their houses. Others cover their embarrassment with humorous signs like "A clean desk is a sign of a sick mind."

Many paperholics end up paying unnecessary service charges and tax penalties or having their utilities cut off because they couldn't find or complete the paperwork. Paperholics constantly make excuses for their behavior or deny it. Some rarely go anywhere because they cannot enjoy themselves until their paperwork is finished—and it never is. Others never stay at home to avoid facing the chaos. Marriage and family relationships suffer seriously when the paperholic's clutter intrudes on others.

Who Are the Paperholics?

At the end of virtually every presentation I give, at least one person, and often many people, share

REAL-LIFE PAPERHOLICS

- An internationally recognized medical researcher asked me to help organize his office. When I arrived, we literally rolled piles of paper out of his office on his chair to make room for me to stand!
- A woman called and told me she hadn't had anyone in her home for over ten years. The reason? Paper piled on every flat surface, stuffed in shopping bags under the bed and shoved in all available drawer and cupboard space. Her children tried to help, but every attempt turned into an emotional disaster. The situation came to a head when the condominium management called the fire department.

stories of the people they know, and often love, who suffer from this problem. They come from all walks of life, and often appear totally together in their professional lives. Paperholics can be people of any age. A paperholic is someone to whom every piece of paper represents an opportunity, an obligation, a threat, a memory or a dream. Paperholics keep piles of articles in case they need to prove a position on a particular issue. They hold on to newspapers because they haven't had time to read or clip the articles. The irony is that usually they cannot find the articles when they want them; sometimes they don't even realize that they have them.

There is nothing wrong with keeping every greeting card and letter you've ever received, if you have plenty of space and it brings you pleasure. If, however, your daily living is impeded because of papers out of the past, you need to examine your actions. The reason and degree of attachment and the ability to let go due to new circumstances distinguishes between normal and pathological saving. Psychologists have studied people referred to as packrats. The psychologists believe that, for some, the problem is a result of an early childhood trauma—a significant loss of some kind. For many people,

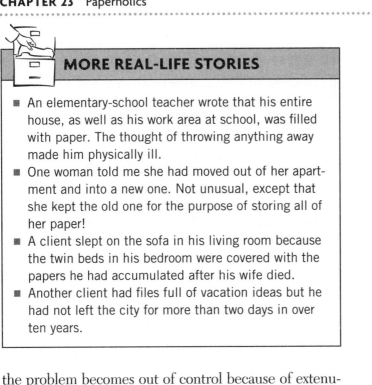

MORE REAL-LIFE STORIES

- An elementary-school teacher wrote that his entire house, as well as his work area at school, was filled with paper. The thought of throwing anything away made him physically ill.
- One woman told me she had moved out of her apartment and into a new one. Not unusual, except that she kept the old one for the purpose of storing all of her paper!
- A client slept on the sofa in his living room because the twin beds in his bedroom were covered with the papers he had accumulated after his wife died.
- Another client had files full of vacation ideas but he had not left the city for more than two days in over ten years.

the problem becomes out of control because of extenuating circumstances, such as ill health, renovating or moving, family crisis, or loss of a job. All the causes of this behavior are not clearly identified, but most savers are not pathological hoarders, just people who need training and support.

People who have the most difficulty managing paper are often the people who generate the most paper. They feel compelled to make duplicate copies so they will be sure to find at least one. Many order information booklets from every available source—even on subjects that may not relate to their lives. They tend to take advantage of every offer for a free magazine issue, fully intending to cancel the subscription later. They take copious notes on any available piece of paper. They pick up information brochures and articles wherever they go. They often subscribe to more magazines and newspapers than they could ever possibly read—and end up reading few of them.

In the end, paperholics live in a vicious cycle. The more paper they accumulate, the less able they are to manage it, and the more out of control they feel.

If You Are a Paperholic

It's essential that you admit you have a problem. Recognize that change does not happen instantaneously. Shelves overflowing with books and outdated magazines, boxes of paper and paper-shuffling habits accumulated over years won't disappear overnight. Behavior patterns take time to unlearn and relearn. Paper-management skills do not come naturally to everyone.

One of the most frequently asked questions that professional organizers hear is, "Why is it so difficult for me to let go of all this stuff?" The answer is not a simple one. Not much formal study has been given to the problem, although it is one from which many suffer.

Accept the fact that you cannot undo what you may now feel are mistakes. Take the advice in this book and start over with today's papers. Ignore the backlog for now. Create a place to work that you find pleasant. Set up your paper-management center (as described in Chapter 3) to handle today's paper. Keep asking yourself the question, "What is the worst possible thing that would happen if I didn't have this piece of paper?" Begin to imagine how you will feel when you are successful. What will your house look like? What things will you do that you aren't doing now?

Even if you read all the guidelines in this book, if you are a true paperholic it is unlikely that you will make the dramatic changes you want to make without assistance of some kind. It is essential to find people you trust to help you. Here are several possibilities:

- **A self-help support group in your area.** Two excellent organizations that offer newsletters, publications, and information about support groups are:

   Messies Anonymous
   5025 S.W. 114th Avenue
   Miami, FL 33165
   800-637-7292
   www.messies.com

NSGCD (National Study Group on
Chronic Disorganization)
1142 Chatsworth Drive
Avondale Estates, GA 30002
916-962-6227
www.nsgcd.org

- ■ **A mental-health professional** to help you deal with
  such psychological issues as why you need to hang on
  to all that paper.
- ■ **An organizing consultant** who will work with you to go
  through the paper piece by piece (Chapter 24 has
  more information).
- ■ **A very special nonjudgmental friend** or relative who
  will work with you or encourage and support you. (I
  must add that such a person is often not easy to find.)
- ■ **A combination of any** or all of the above.

If Someone You Love Is a Paperholic

If someone you know or love is a paperholic, you may
be asking "What can I do?" Truthfully, maybe nothing.
It's easy for us to be critical of others who find it difficult
to do what we do easily, and it's important to accept that
correcting the situation will require much more than
simply applying self-discipline.

Sometimes letting a paperholic know that other
people have similar difficulties can be a great relief. One
of the most common reactions to the scenarios I present
in paper-management seminars is, "When did you see
my house?"

Perhaps the most important lesson that I have
learned about living with a paperholic is the importance of defining boundaries. If possible, negotiate
with that person regarding what papers (magazines,
newspapers, photos, etc.) are acceptable in shared
spaces. Identify other areas of your home where he or

> **Perhaps the most important lesson I have learned about living with a paperholic is the importance of defining boundaries.**

she can accumulate paper according to his or her own wishes. When the papers begin to spill into other areas, you then have a right to take steps to correct the problem. Communication is a key issue. Often it takes time and practice, as well as professional assistance, to master effective techniques.

Finally, acknowledge that all of us have issues we need to resolve. Concentrate on your own issues and allow the paperholic to solve his or her own problem.

Caging That Tiger

t this point, a review of the basic components of this paper-management system is in order. Keep in mind that every piece of paper in your life can be categorized and put into one of seven places:

- **To-Sort Tray**
- **Wastebasket**
- **Calendar**
- **To-Do list**
- **Action Files**
- **Rotary card file/phone book**
- **Reference Files**

Every time you find a pile of papers that requires decisions, ask yourself these questions about each piece:

- "Can this be recycled or go in the wastebasket?"
- If not, "Do I need to make an appointment with myself to do something?" If so, enter the information in your calendar.
- "Does this piece of paper require action or recall by me at some yet-undetermined time in the future?" If so, enter it in your to-do list.
- "Are there any addresses, telephone numbers, or pieces of mini information that I should put on my rotary phone-file or in my computer database?"
- If you entered the information in any of the above places, "Do I still need to keep the piece of paper?" If so, "Does this piece of paper require action or am I keeping it for reference?"
- If the paper requires action, "What specific action do I

need to take?" The answer will tell you into which Action File you should put it.

- If I am keeping the paper for reference, "What word would I think of if I wanted this piece of paper again?" The answer will tell you into what Reference File you should put it.

Getting Rid of the Boxes

In the question and answer period following one of my speeches, a woman asked, "I have four large packing boxes full of papers that I have been telling myself for three years I will organize 'one of these days,' but each time I try I am totally overwhelmed. What can I do?"

I told her that I could think of only two options for getting rid of the boxes: Decide that since she survived for three years without any of the information in them she could take a deep breath and toss them all in the trash; or go through the papers one by one using the system described in this book, making decisions about each piece of paper.

You have the same choices for dealing with your accumulated papers. It may help you determine which option you want to choose to know that going through the equivalent of one vertical-file cabinet drawer takes about four hours. If the peace of mind you will get from going through the papers is worth hours of your time, by all means make an appointment with yourself to do it as soon as possible. If spending that time in some other way is more important, then throw the boxes away immediately. If you find yourself postponing the decision, ask yourself, "What am I going to know tomorrow that I don't know today?"

Just Get Started

At this point, one of the major questions you may have is "How long will it take?" You cannot expect to solve all of your paper-management problems overnight. Don't worry how long it will take. Just get started. One of the most exciting things you will discover is that what you learn in organizing one area of your life will carry over into other areas. As you enjoy your successes, you will be encouraged to keep going.

Keep It Growing

There are no magic wands. No matter how terrific the system you develop, it will not maintain itself, and it will not last forever. If after reading this book, or even parts of it, you have to admit that you are not willing to do what needs to be done, then your assignment is to determine who will help you and how.

Keep in mind, however, that the key issue in any paper-management system is decision making. You will either have to make the decisions yourself or give the person to whom you delegate your paper management the authority to make those decisions. A successful system will probably require a combination of decision making and delegation.

Many times clients will call me because a system they have established is not working. Nine times out of 10, the problem is not that the system was bad but that they have outgrown the system. Personal paper-management is an ongoing process. It will need to change as you change. If your priorities, your support system, your space availability or your family situation change, you may need to adjust your system to fit those changes.

Call for Action

If you have read this book and still don't know how to create an effective system or want additional support or assistance for your specific needs, you have several options. Read through the following questions and answers to see what they are:

I'd like to talk to you, are you available? Contact me— I'd love to hear from you. Feel free to call, write or e-mail me at Hemphill Productivity Institute, Inc., 1464 Garner Station Blvd., #330, Raleigh, NC 27603-3634.

continued on page 186

RECORDS RETENTION GUIDE

Throughout this book I've written about different kinds of paper that you need to keep—or might want to keep. This retention guide will serve as a quick reference tool for you to use to identify your papers and note where you keep them and how long they need to be retained. Check the index for references to detailed discussions about ways to deal with the various documents. Then fill out the worksheet, and keep it in a handy location. Also make copies for people in your life who might need the information in case of an emergency.

In many cases, it's up to you where you want to keep a document and how long you decide to hold on to it. I've indicated a specific location and/or retention guideline where there is a legal requirement—or I've felt it would be helpful to do so.

Keep in mind that where you keep the documents is not nearly as important as

DOCUMENT	LOCATION	RETAIN HOW LONG
Education Records		
Certificates	_____	_____
Diplomas	_____	_____
Letters of reference	_____	Update periodically
Resumes	_____	Until superseded
Health Records		
Illness records	_____	Permanently
Vaccination Records	_____	Permanently
Insurance		
Automobile	_____	Statute of limitations (in case of late claims)
Disability	_____	Duration of policy
Health	_____	Duration of policy
Homeowner's	_____	Statute of limitation (in case of late claims)
Liability	_____	Statute of limitations (in case of late claims)
Life	Safe deposit box	Duration of policy
Personal property	_____	Duration of policy
Umbrella policy	_____	Duration of policy

doing it consistently. Problems develop when part of the information you need is in one location and part is in another. However, because of space considerations, it may sometimes be necessary to put documents in more than one place. When this happens, be sure to note both locations on this guide. For example, old tax records could be stored in the attic while the most recent year's records could be in your Reference File.

Be sure to include a timetable for transferring records from active to inactive storage or disposal. (A good time to do this would be after you file your tax return.) You may find that the least complicated method for keeping records is to put all records for a given year into a large envelope or box and store them in chronological order. When you put in the latest year's records, take out unneeded or unwanted material from earlier years.

Investments

Purchase records	_____	As long as you own a security, then keep with sale record
Sales records	_____	Six years after sale, for tax purposes
Major home improvements	_____	As long as you own, then with tax records
Collectibles	_____	As long as you own, then with tax records
Household inventory	_____	Update annually
Mortgage information	_____	6 years after sale

Military records

Discharge papers	Safe deposit box	Permanently

Personal-property records

Automobile registration	Copy in car, original with driver	As long as you own auto
Receipts for major purchases	_____	As long as you own item

continued on page 186

RECORDS RETENTION GUIDE (continued)

Personal life

Calendars (past)	_____	_____
Directories	_____	_____
Letters/greeting cards received	_____	_____
Memorabilia	_____	_____
Photographs	_____	_____
Religious records	_____	_____

Pet records

_____ _____ _____

Tax and Financial

Bank statements	_____	6 years
Canceled checks	_____	6 years, if for deductible item
Certificates of deposit	_____	Until cashed in
Contracts	_____	6 years after completion
Credit card statements/receipts	_____	6 years, if for deductible item
Income-tax returns	_____	Generally 6 years. Exception: non-deductible IRA form (indefinitely)
Income-tax support	_____	Same as above documents
Loan agreements	_____	6 years after payment
Loan payment books	_____	Until paid

My phone number is 800–427–0237, and my e-mail address is barbara@ProductiveEnvironment.com.

It seems that in this age of high technology, information changes so fast. How can I stay current? I frequently add updates to my Web site, in addition to new resources, free downloadable articles, surveys and more. So visit www.ProductiveEnvironment.com often, bookmark the site, or better yet sign up for the free e-zine and stay informed. Look for book-specific updates in the section

Pension-plan records	_____	Generally keep current year only
Rental contracts	_____	As long as in effect
Pay stub	_____	Until W-2 confirmed
Trust agreements	_____	As long as in effect

Vital records

Adoption papers	Safe deposit box	Permanently
Automobile title	Safe deposit box	As long as you own auto
Birth certificates	Safe deposit box	Permanently
Citizenship papers	Safe deposit box	Permanently
Copyrights/Patents	Safe deposit box	As long as in effect
Death certificates	Safe deposit box	Until estate is settled
Divorce decrees	Safe deposit box	Permanently
Letter of last instructions	_____	Permanently. Update as needed
Marriage certificate	Safe deposit box	Permanently
Passports	_____	Keep current
Power of attorney	_____	Permanently. Update as needed
Safe deposit box key	_____	As long as you keep box
Safe deposit box inventory	_____	Update regularly
Social security records	_____	Permanently
Wills	_____	As long as valid
Warranties & instructions	_____	As long as you own appliance or device

marked "Taming the Paper Tiger at Home."

Who else can help me? Check your phone book's classified pages under Organizing Consultants or Personal Services to find someone who specializes in setting up systems for paper management. Contact NAPO (National Association for Professional Organizers) at www.napo.net for a list of organizers in your area. Paper Tiger Authorized Consultants, or PTACs, are a team of productivity professionals who have gone through extensive training

WHAT AN ORGANIZING CONSULTANT OFFERS

The first step in developing a good working relationship with an organizing consultant is to have a realistic understanding of what particular services that consultant offers. Although every organizing consultant is different, you can and should expect:

- **complete confidentiality;**
- **open discussion** about the cost of services;
- **appointments scheduled** to meet your professional or personal needs;
- **an ability to apply** the "principles of organization" to your particular situation;
- **expertise and experience** in the "principles of organization" applied to personal and professional life;
- **creative and innovative** problem solving; and
- **availability** and a continued interest in your situation, should you desire.

Some organizing consultants specialize in hands-on assistance, which may include:

- **a willingness** to do whatever task needs to be done in the interest of achieving mutually determined goals;
- **physical assistance,** as well as verbal instruction. A willingness to do whatever you would do—including getting dirty;
- **shopping assistance** if you need or want it; and
- **assistance in finding** another professional resource if it is appropriate or desirable.

There are hundreds of organizing consultants in the country, and more are being trained everyday. The exciting aspect of the industry is the networking that takes place among the organizers themselves. Not all organizers provide the same services, so keep looking until you find the one that suits your needs and your personality.

by me to convert clients to the Paper Tiger System. You can find out if there's a consultant in your area by checking the Web site, www.ProductiveEnvironment.com.

How do I work with a consultant? Many people procrastinate about making an appointment with an organizing consultant. They're often stuck with the "clean up before the maid comes" syndrome, or they are concerned about how to prepare for the organizing consultant's arrival.

Put aside any worries about needing to justify your situation. The organizing consultant's role is to provide professional advice, not to make judgments. Ask yourself the questions: "Why did I make this appointment with an organizing consultant?" and "What do I want to change?"

It is not necessary to do anything, but if you feel a need to get started before the consultant comes, here are some suggestions.

- **Choose where you would like to begin**—with today's mail or the attic—so you're ready to begin when the consultant arrives. .
- **Gather together any supplies** you may have on hand that will be helpful in the organizing process—file folders, labels, marking pens, boxes, containers, wastebaskets, etc.
- **Put all like things together**—banking information, photographs, magazines, etc.
- **Relax!** If you're unsure about where to begin or what to do, your organizing consultant has the knowledge and experience to guide you in making that decision.

What If It's Not Me That Needs Organizing, It's My Family?

A note of caution: It is always easier to see what someone else needs to do than it is to see what we need to do. In teaching organizing skills to families, one of my key roles is to insure that family members concentrate on solving their own organizing problems instead of what other family members need to do. As you read this book and experiment with developing new paper-management systems for yourself, resist the urge to insist that other people join you. Many of the systems you develop will automatically make paper management easier for other people, but let them discover it for themselves!

Although you are at the end of this book, you are at the beginning of a new adventure in learning to control the paper in your life. Remember, "In every organizing process, things will get worse before they get better." Try to remain optimistic. Forgive yourself when you see the mistakes you have made in the past and move on. Feeling guilty does not help anything. Be willing to ask for help when you need it, and reward yourself for each accomplishment along the way. Now grab that tiger by the tail! You are on your way to a personal paper-management system that works for you!

Index